Spain in the West Series

XV

José María Narbaez

José Narváez
The Forgotten Explorer

Including His Narrative of a Voyage on the Northwest Coast in 1788

by

Jim McDowell

THE ARTHUR H. CLARK COMPANY
Spokane, Washington
1998

Arthur H. Clark Company
P.O. Box 14707
Spokane, WA 99214

Library of Congress Catalog Card Number 97-6599
ISBN-0-87062-265-x

Library of Congress Cataloging-in-Publication Data

McDowell, Jim, 1934-
José Narváez : the forgotten explorer / by Jim McDowell.
p. 192 cm. —(Spain in the West series ; 15)
Includes bibliographical references and index.
ISBN 0-87062-265-x (alk. paper)
1. Narváez, José, b. 1768? 2. Northwest Coast of North America--Discovery and exploration—Spanish. 3. Explorers—Northwest Coast of North America—Biography. 4. Explorers—Spain—Biography.
I. Title. II. Series: Spain in the West ; 15.
F851.5.M43 1998
910'.92—dc21 97-6599
[B] CIP

Frontispiece: Signed portrait of Don José Maria Narváez (1768–1840) done in 1830s. At age 23, he discovered the present site of Vancouver and charted Georgia Strait in July 1791. *Courtesy of Gabriel Agraz Garcia.* The signature sample is copied from the journal of 1778.

CONTENTS

Illustrations

Introduction

The voyages of early European mariners in small sailing vessels, their quests for new trade routes, and their encounters with strangers in unknown lands remain a touchstone of identity for North Americans. Even in our complex age of high technology, global markets, and multiculturalism, the exploits of these voyagers still capture our imagination. This book is about one of those men—a Spanish-Mexican mariner whose full life story has never been told. Yet he made some of the most significant discoveries during the age of exploration on America's North Pacific coast.

In 1788, José María Narváez y Gervete, a young Spanish navigator, was the first Spaniard to reconnoiter a functioning Russian fur trading outpost in the North Pacific. Between 1789 and 1791, he was the first European to probe Juan de Fuca Strait, sail across the large inland sea of Georgia Strait, explore its numerous islands, and discover the site of what is now western Canada's largest city—Vancouver, British Columbia.

Until now, other mariners have tended to receive credit for these achievements. Most historians have recognized the controversial Captain José Martínez for making Spain's first contact with the Russians when he led an expedition to Alaskan waters in 1788. But Narváez' journal of that voyage, which the author has translated into English for the first time, shows they were incorrect.

It is curious that Juan de Fuca Strait—the long-sought western entrance to the legendary Northwest Passage that would supposedly link the Atlantic and Pacific Oceans—went unexplored as long as it did. The renowned Captain James Cook, who investigated so much of the Pacific for England, sailed right past the fog-shrouded Strait in 1778. The first recorded sighting was made in 1787 by a woman: Mrs. Charles William Barkley, wife of the American fur trader who captained the *American Eagle*.[1] But exploration of the Strait was left to Narváez. In 1789, he charted its interior for the first time.

The mariner commonly given credit for exploring Georgia Strait and discovering the site of the city that now bears his name is Britain's ace surveyor, Captain George Vancouver, aboard the large square-rigged *HMS Discovery* in 1792. But Narváez sailed the same waters one year earlier as an uncelebrated 23-year-old pilot in command of a small sloop and longboat.

Today the young explorer's remarkable achievements are either unknown or almost forgotten and his biography remains unfamiliar to most North Americans. The fame attained by the British captains Cook and Vancouver for their explorations of the Pacific Northwest coast in the late 1700s has overshadowed the achievements of Spanish naval officers during the same period. Few have been overlooked more than Narváez. England trumpeted the isolated voyages of its two famous explorers. But the Spanish officers and their largely Mexican crews, who did far more work, won little recognition outside Madrid. Spain had no interest in supplying the world with information about the area. She was more intent on retaining the entire Pacific coast of North America as her territory and possibly being the first to find the fabled Northwest Passage.

[1]Lamb, William Kaye, "The Mystery of Mrs. Barkley's Diary," 43.

Captain Vancouver's meticulous explorations of Juan de Fuca Strait, Georgia Strait, and the surrounding coast in 1792 cannot be minimized. But he was not the first to explore those waters, to anchor along those shores, to view the majestic mountains, to trade with the native Indians, nor to name many of the landmarks. The Spaniards preceded him and their stories deserve equal attention. One of them was Narváez, a relatively ignored but noteworthy Spanish mariner. This book tells his story.

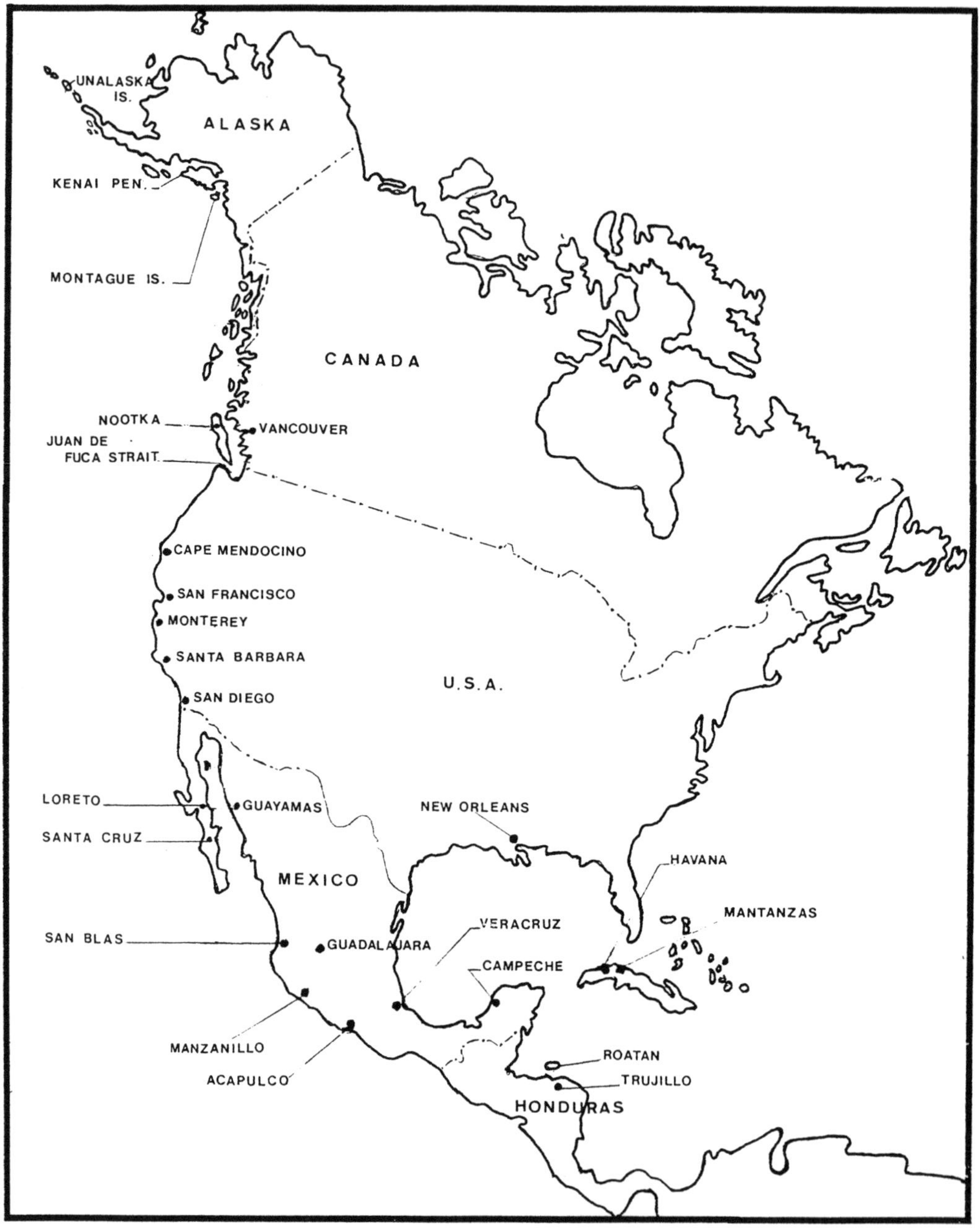
UNALASKA IS.
ALASKA
KENAI PEN.
MONTAGUE IS.
CANADA
NOOTKA
VANCOUVER
JUAN DE FUCA STRAIT
CAPE MENDOCINO
SAN FRANCISCO
MONTEREY
SANTA BARBARA
SAN DIEGO
U.S.A.
LORETO
GUAYAMAS
SANTA CRUZ
NEW ORLEANS
HAVANA
MEXICO
MANTANZAS
SAN BLAS
GUADALAJARA
VERACRUZ
CAMPECHE
MANZANILLO
ACAPULCO
ROATAN
TRUJILLO
HONDURAS

CHAPTER 1

From Cádiz to New Spain

José María Narváez was born in 1768[1] in Cádiz, a bustling port city in southwestern Spain, about 50 miles northwest of the entrance to the Mediterranean Sea. His parents, Antonio Narváez and Urzula Gervete, had lived in the clean, beautiful town all their lives. It was situated at the tip of Isla de Leon (now San Fernando)—a narrow peninsula joined to the mainland by the Suazo bridge.

Because of its cleanliness, the natives called Cádiz *"Tacita de Plata"* ("Little Cup of Silver"). Tracing its history back 3,000 years to a Phoenician settlement in 1100 B.C., Cádiz now lays claim to being Europe's oldest continually inhabited town. The development of trade with the Indies brought prosperity to the city, which reached its zenith during the eighteenth century, supplanting Seville as Spain's chief port and its most important naval base.

Determined to regain its position as a naval power, the Spanish crown concentrated a significant portion of its expenditures between 1700 and 1790 on rebuilding a modern navy from scratch. In 1726, it started construction of La Car-

[1]The author has been unable to obtain Narváez' actual date of birth. The record presents conflicting years of birth, ranging from 1756 (Narváez' Naval record) to 1771 (*Apendice al Diccionario Universal de Historia y de Geografía).* The year 1768 used herein is based on Narváez' testimony before a military tribunal held in Tepic, Mexico, on February 13, 1811, when he stated that he was 43 years old. (See: Cardenas de la Peña, Enrique. *San Blas de Nayarit.* Vol. 2, p. 117.

raca royal shipyard in Cádiz. Along with fully-integrated facilities at Santander and Cartagena, La Carraca became one of the country's first three large ship-building sites on the mainland. In 1732, La Carraca launched its first of seven *navios* (battleships). By 1790, the three yards would construct 64 such ships of the line. But Havana, which turned out 74 *navios* during the period, was by far the largest producer. Altogether, Spain built or acquired 227 ships of the line by the turn of the century. But its shipyards also turned out scores of smaller ships. By 1794, when the Spanish Navy reached its nadir, it contained a total active force of 79 *navios,* 53 frigates, 52 smaller warships, and 51 supply ships.[2]

As a child Narváez played on the shores of Isla de Leon, where he enjoyed long hours watching sailing ships of all types come and go along the fishhook curve of Cádiz Bay. On a stormy day, the Atlantic Ocean sent waves crashing over the sea wall in great surges of white power, soaking anyone who ventured too close. The boy's greatest thrill was seeing one of the new three-decked wooden warships leave port under full sail, flags flying, with hundreds of sailors on board.

But the most important event each year along the Coast of Light was the *almadraba* (tuna fishery). In late spring, Atlantic tuna fish heading for the Mediterranean swung close inshore just south of Cádiz. For ages, the annual *almadraba* was conducted in two stages. In the first, fishermen in boats drove the tuna toward the beach and shallow lagoons of Conil, about 25 miles south of Cádiz. There trumpeters in a tower summoned people who hauled large net pens to trap the fish. In the second phase, the trapped tuna were speared, hauled ashore with gaffs, and loaded on carts. It often took four or five men to beach a flailing tuna. On shore, the fish were butchered and prepared for sale. Some were sold fresh, but most were salted, dried, and barreled.

---

[2]Harbron, John, *Trafalgar and the Spanish Navy*, p. 15-42.

Narváez was a bright youngster. On April 23, 1782, at the age of 14, he won acceptance to the Royal (Naval) Academy for midshipmen on nearby Isla de Leon.[3] Four months later, Narváez went to sea as an unpaid apprentice[4] aboard the 70-74 gun *navio Triunfante.*[5] He saw his first combat October 20, 1782, with the combined Spanish and French squadron. It was commanded by Admiral of the Fleet Luis de Cordova, one of Spain's most aggressive naval commanders of that era. From that fall to the following spring, Admiral Cordova's fleet battled the English navy between the Straits of Gibraltar and Cape Saint Vincent in Portugal. On January 2, 1783, Narváez was appointed *tercer piloto havilitado* ("qualified third pilot"). The rank of *piloto* in the Spanish Armada was junior to an *alférez* (ensign), which in turn was junior to a *teniente* (lieutenant)—usually considered the lowest rank of *oficial del mar* (commissioned officer). Narváez had begun his slow climb up the promotional ladder.[6]

The British fleet was commanded by Admiral Richard Earl Howe, who is heralded for his brilliant last-ditch effort to escort a supply convoy into Gibraltar while it was under siege. Howe's allegedly brilliant tactics won the day. But returning

[3] At that time, the midshipmen's school at Cádiz (founded in 1717) concentrated on a short course of practical instruction for trained pilots, not scientific officers, because the Navy needed a steady supply of such leaders for its war activities. In 1783, Vicente Tofiño developed a four-month course of advanced studies that was aimed at training an elite corps of officers who would be expert astronomers and scientists. As Narváez only attended the former program, he would learn most of his advanced hydrographic skills on the job.

[4] Marina de Guerra, *Estado de los méritos y servicios del Primer Piloto, Graduado de Alferez de Navio de la Real Armada Don José María Narváez*..., p. 1.

[5] The *Triunfante* was launched in Ferrol, Spain in 1756 and wrecked off Rosas, Spain in 1795. (See: Harbron, op. cit., p. 169.)

[6] From *piloto de segunda clase* (second pilot), *piloto de primera clase* (first pilot), *alferez de fragata* (frigate ensign) *and alferez de navio* (ship's ensign), a mariner aspired to *teniente de fragata* (frigate lieutenant). But few former pilots achieved that rank.

Commissioned officers graduated from marine academies as *tenientes de fragata*. They aspired to the ranks of *teniente de navio* (ship's lieutenant), *capitan de fragata* (frigate captain) and *capitan de navio* (ship's captain). The chief officer of a Spanish ship was the *comandante*, regardless of rank. The *piloto* was the mate, the *pilotin* was the pilot's mate. (See: Cook, Warren, *Flood Tide of Empire*, fn. 29, p.55.)

to England, Howe found his 33 poorly equipped, undermanned ships to leeward of 46 battle-ready enemy vessels, which had him outgunned. The Spanish, however, made a strategic mistake. Instead of attacking Howe from their windward position, the Spaniards only fired some shots from long range. Howe sailed off without damage. Known popularly as "Black Dick," the British admiral served as First Lord of the Admiralty from 1783-88. (Ironically, one of the major fjords that Narváez would discover nine years later in the Pacific Northwest and name *Carmelo* was renamed Howe Sound by Captain Vancouver.)

Promoted to a *tercer piloto de numero* ("third pilot") October 1, 1783, Narváez sailed to Constantinople (now Istanbul) and Cartagena. In 1784, he journeyed to New Spain. His first assignment was Havana. During the next three years he served aboard supply ships to the ports of Veracruz, New Orleans, Mantanzas (Cuba), Campeche (Mexico), Roatan, and Trujillo (Honduras). At sea almost continuously, he went without the standard fifteen-day annual vacation for three years.[7] On November 1, 1787 he was promoted to *segundo piloto havilitado* (qualified second pilot) and assigned, along with four other pilots, to the small San Blas naval station about 75 miles north of what is now Puerto Vallarta on Mexico's west coast.

The 20-year-old mariner arrived in San Blas on February 4, 1788. The busy port, which played a key role in the early history of the Californias and the Pacific Northwest coast, owed its importance to a naval station and supply base, established there in 1768.[8] The town was a small hamlet built on a promontory about 150 feet high, which rose out of a low swampy plain at the mouth of the San Pedro River.

---

[7]Marina de Guerra, op. cit., p. 2.

[8]See: Thurman, Michael E. *The Naval Department of San Blas.*

Almost a century later, on March 15, 1882, the grim, mediocre little port would inspire the romantic American poet Henry Wadsworth Longfellow to paint a nostalgic picture when he wrote his last poem.

The Bells of San Blas

What say the Bells of San Blas
To the ships that southward pass
   From the harbor of Mazatlán?
To them it is nothing more
Than the sound of surf on the shore,—
   Nothing more to master or man.

But to me, a dreamer of dreams,
To whom what is and what seems
   Are often one and the same,—
The Bells of San Blas to me
Have a strange, wild melody,
   And are something more than a name.

For bells are the voice of the church;
They have tones that touch and search
   The hearts of young and old;
One sound to all, yet each
Lends a meaning to their speech,
   And the meaning is manifold.

They are a voice of the Past,
Of an age that is fading fast,
   Of a power austere and grand,
When the flag of Spain unfurled
Its folds o'er this western world,
   And the Priest was lord of the land.

The chapel that once looked down
On the little seaport town
   Has crumbled into dust;
And on oaken beams below
The bells swing to and fro,
   And are green with mold and rust.

"Is, then, the old faith dead,"
They say, "and in its stead
   Is some new faith proclaimed,
That we are forced to remain
Naked to sun and rain,
   Unsheltered and ashamed?

"Once, in our tower aloof,
We rang over wall and roof
   Our warnings and our complaints;
And round about us there
The white doves filled the air,
   Like the white souls of the saints.

"The saints! Ah, have they grown
Forgetful of their own?
   Are they asleep, or dead,
That open to the sky
Their ruined Missions lie,
   No longer tenanted?

"Oh, bring us back once more
The varnished days of yore,
   When the world with faith was filled;
Bring back the fervid zeal,
The hearts of fire and steel,
   The hands that believe and build.

"Then from our tower again
We will send over land and main
   Our voices of command,
Like exiled kings who return
To their thrones, and the people learn
   That the Priest is lord of the land!"

O Bells of San Blas, in vain
Ye call back the Past again;
   The Past is deaf to your prayer!
Out of the shadows of night
The world rolls into light;
   It is daybreak everywhere.

By the time Narváez arrived at San Blas, it had reached peak activity as a supply base for all Spanish ships in the North Pacific, including those making exploration voyages. It also supplied New Spain's missions at San Diego and Monterey, which had been set up as safe havens for treasure-laden galleons returning annually from Manila. Two batteries guarded the harbor, which included a marine station, arsenal, warehouses, and offices. The naval department at San Blas faced several difficulties: chronic shortages of suitable ships and officers, physical isolation from major population centers, a baneful climate, and a dearth of readily available marine equipment. The base was costly to maintain, but it would become fundamental for launching Spain's last major expansion in America—the maritime exploration, exploitation, and settlement of the ocean frontier from California to Alaska.[9]

Geographically, the harbor had several advantages, but for ships it was not an ideal anchorage. By 1779, it had started to fill up with sand, so the department had been thinking for years about moving its headquarters to the excellent port of Acapulco. But that harbor lacked immediate sources of lumber needed for ship construction.

"It [San Blas] has the great defect of not being more than an estuary, incapable of receiving boats that are more than twelve feet [draft]," Narváez would write in 1822, when the Mexican Navy commissioned him to find a better location.[10] Most ships were forced to anchor outside the estuary, where they were protected from mild northeasterly winds during the summer. "But it doesn't happen that way when the season of the rains comes in, which make it indispensably necessary to

[9]For background, see Thurman, op. cit.

[10]Narváez, José María, "Report about the Coasts of the South Sea," *The Political and Literary Weekly of Mexico,* Vol. 4, Numbers 12 and 13, 1822 (transcribed by Garcia, Gabriel Agraz, *Un Gaditano Insigne en America,* p. 36.)

abandon [the port] and go to the port of Guaymas on the coast of Sonora," wrote Narváez. "But [San Blas] has the advantage of the exquisite and abundant trees for construction that are produced nearby and can be transported very easily at a small cost on the Santiago River."

In 1788, young Narváez was handed the first of a series of challenging assignments that made him navigator on voyages of discovery and mapping along the northern coast above Baja and Alta California. For the next seven years, he would be involved as a junior officer in all the major events of Spain's exploration of the Pacific Northwest.

One month after arriving in San Blas, Narváez departed on his first voyage northward. From early March to late October of 1788, he sailed to America's northwest coast as pilot to Gonzalo López de Haro aboard the packetboat *San Carlos*.[11] It was the fourth voyage by Spaniards to the northern waters and the first of two important but careless expeditions led by Estevan José Martínez. For two years, Narváez' destiny would be tied to the erratic, violent, and irresponsible escapades of this contentious second-rate explorer. Beyond middle age, Martínez had not even achieved the rank of a commissioned officer. But he was the most experienced pilot left in San Blas, where he had been stationed for at least fifteen years. All the first rank officers located at San Blas had been assigned elsewhere. To his credit, Martínez was a dedicated, patriotic navy man, who was enthusiastic about extending Spain's settlement northward. But he was short-tempered, imprudent, and not above using deception to achieve personal and political ends.

Dealing with that deceit as a fledgling naval officer would pose severe tests for Narváez' sense of responsibility, his respect for military discipline, and his diplomatic skills.

[11]Probably built in Havana in 1772. (See: Harbron, op. cit., 52- 53.)

ENGRAVING OF INDIAN VILLAGE AT FRIENDLY COVE (YUQUOT).
Sketch by John Webber, 1778. *Courtesy of Vancouver Public Library.*

CHAPTER 2

The Russian "Threat"

In the early 1700s, Russian expansion across Siberia led to a maritime expedition ordered by Tsar Peter the Great. It was commanded by the Danish navigator Vitus Bering, who was assisted by the Russian captain Aleksei Chirikov. In 1728, the two men explored the Kamchatka Peninsula and the open sea between Asia and America that would carry Bering's name. In 1741 Bering and Chirikov investigated the Aleutian Islands and the Alaskan coast, confirming the absence of a temperate passage between the Pacific and the Atlantic. Their voyages also opened the north Pacific coast to the lucrative fur trade. By 1763, Russian traders reached Kodiak. The Aleuts[1] drove them away, but the Russians returned 21 years later under the command of the famous fur trader Grigorii Shelikhov. They established the first European settlement in Alaska at Three Saints Bay.

About 20,000 Aleuts lived on Kodiak when the foreigners arrived. A few months after landing at Three Saints Bay, Shelikhov decided to subdue the natives and force them to hunt sea otters for his company. The commander led 70 armed men in skin boats east from Kodiak to a large headland on what is now Sitkalidak Island, where about 2,000 Aleuts had sought safety. Steep cliffs made what would be called Refuge Rock inaccessible from the seaward side. On the other side, the

[1]Now called Alutiiq.

promontory was connected to Sitkalidak Island at the head of Partition Cove by a narrow land bridge, which was underwater most of the time. At low tide, the Russians crossed the thin spit, charged onto the headland, killed hundreds of Aleuts, and took about 500 of them as hostages or slaves. The massacre broke the back of Aleut resistance.[2]

By 1786, the Spanish government had grown alarmed at reports of four Russian outposts in Alaska and one in Puerto de Nuca (Nootka). More ominous, Britain's famous voyager Captain James Cook had met with the Russians at Unalaska. To find out what was going on, Madrid ordered two ships dispatched from San Blas. The frigate *Princesa,* commanded by Martínez, and the storeship *San Carlos,* with Narváez aboard, set sail March 8, 1788. Their objective was reconnaissance, not settlement, of the coast of Alaska between 60°N and 61°N of latitude. Narváez kept a brief journal of the voyage, recording in his stylish handwriting elementary navigational information, some interesting personal observations, and considerable valuable intelligence about Russian activities. Along with the explanations that accompany it, this previously untranslated log constitutes, in certain respects, a first contact document and it reveals some unappreciated discoveries made by this pilot.[3]

Despite mounting disputes between the pilots and Commander Martínez over actual locations, the explorers reached the Alaskan coast. On May 16, Narváez sighted Montague Island and the entrance to Prince William Sound. On June 11, while reconnoitering Montague Island, Narváez found a large building which he later learned was a Russian outpost. This was Spain's first hard evidence of the Russians' presence.

[2] Eliot, John L., "Alaska's Island Refuge," p. 53.

[3] Narváez, José María. *Diario . . . , 1788.* See author's translation: Narrative of the Voyage, 1788, which constitutes chapter nine.

But full exploration of Prince William Sound—one of the expedition's prime objectives—was aborted by a stormy and prolonged quarrel about altering logs to conform with the Commander's records.[4] Martínez became so abusive toward his subordinates that his second in command, López de Haro eventually headed westward on his own toward Trinidad Island (Trinity Islands). On June 28, the *San Carlos* approached the southeast shore of Kodiak Island, where the Spaniards traded with 12 canoes of Indians. The natives had clearly been trading with some European nation. They also carried several small scraps of paper bearing Russian writing, one of which was dated 1784. López de Haro got the impression these were vouchers for payment of tribute.[5] The Spaniard was eager to obtain these first indisputable signs of Russian presence. He cleverly swapped trinkets with the Indians for their vouchers.[6]

On June 30, López de Haro sent Narváez in an armed longboat to reconnoiter the Russian trading post at Three Saints Bay, Kodiak Island. Narváez became the first Spaniard to make contact with a large contingent of Russians[7] when he met Evstrat Delarov, commander of the settlement, which had been established in 1784 by Shelikhov. Narváez brought Delarov back to the *San Carlos* with three other Russians. In his journal, Narváez wrote:

> Captain López de Haro gave them a barrel of wine, some chocolate and other things to get them to tell us more [about the extent of their

[4]The Spaniards would not explore the sound until 1790.

[5]The Spaniards later learned that the Indians paid a three ruble head tax and a 10 percent tax on trade. (See: Archer, Christon, *"Russians, Indians & Passages,"* p. 136.)

[6]*Diario de Antonio Serantes,* June 28-30, 1788. Serantes' description is almost identical to the one recorded by Narváez. Between June 29 and July 1, Martínez apparently engaged in a similar exchange of tribute slips for fake receipts. (See: *Diario de Antonio Palacios,* June 30, 1788. Biblioteca Nacional, Mexico.)

[7]On June 27, Martínez met a single Russian lookout when he reached the southernmost point of the Trinity Islands, but he would not visit Potap Kuzmich Zaikov's large establishment at today's Dutch Harbor, Unalaska, until July 21.

occupation]. Captain [Delarov] was most appreciative, and he invited us to come to their establishment inside the port. We accepted the invitation and pulled out our chart of these coasts to see if they would either point out some other establishments or give another name to the Port of Nootka or Prince William Sound. When Captain [Delarov] saw it, he took a pencil and drew a very wide and navigable canal . . ."[west of Kodiak].[8]

On July 1, Narváez became the first Spanish officer to reconnoiter a working Russian outpost. At the end of his visit, Captain Delarov gave Narváez a map of the Alaskan coast, on which he later marked seven Russian outposts containing a total of 462 men and several sloops. Delarov said his country was sending two supply ships to Nootka in 1789 to occupy the port. He also gave the Spaniards a letter dated June 25, 1788, which contained both English and Russian words. The Spaniards couldn't read it, but they copied it. It turned out to be from a British mariner to a Russian fur trader.[9]

In December 1786, the Empress Catherine II had ordered a naval squadron dispatched from the Baltic to the "Eastern Sea" via Cape of Good Hope and Japan. She stated that the expedition's aim was to "safeguard our rights to the lands discovered by Russian seafarers." Captain Grigorii Ivanovich Mulovskii, 29, was selected to command the voyage. His sailing orders included instructions "to take that coast from the harbor of Nootka to the point where Chirikov's discovery [of 1741] begins as possession of the Russian State if no other State is occupying it." But in the late summer of 1787, Turkey and Sweden went to war with Russia. Mulovskii's ships were needed closer to home. The Empress canceled the expedition, ending the Russian bid to win control of America's northwest coast.[10]

---

[8]Narváez, op. cit., entry for June 30-July 1, 1788.

[9]See fn. 75 to Narváez' journal entry for July 1, 1788.

[10]Inglis, Robin. *Spain and the North Pacific Coast,* p. 31-33.

Meanwhile, Martínez had sailed directly to Trinidad (Trinity) Island, where he encountered on June 27 a lone Russian lookout manning an isolated watchtower. Using Indian couriers, the Russian sent a message to Three Saints Bay about the frigate's arrival and it was handed to Narváez on July 1. Having obtained a great deal of vital information from Delarov, López de Haro set sail July 2 and rendezvoused with Martínez the next day at the present Sitkank Island.

Armed with the information supplied by Delarov, the expedition sailed southwestward to investigate the large establishment that the Russians said they maintained on Unalaska Island in the eastern Aleutians. Sailing together July 5, the two ships worked their way along the Alaskan Peninsula, but frequently lost contact with each other. On July 29, Martínez landed on Unalaska Island and anchored off the Russian outpost at the head of Unalaska Inlet. The *San Carlos* did not anchor there until August 4.

Martínez' warship took the outmanned and outgunned Russians by surprise. But Potap Kuzmich Zaikov, commander of the vessel *Sv. Aleksandr Nevskii* put up a good front. Although the head of the Russian trading post had less than 50 men under him, he boasted of commanding 500 and greatly exaggerated the number of Russian outposts in Alaska.[11]

The two parties communicated through Martínez' second pilot Estevan Mondofía, a native of Raguza [modern Dubrovnik, Croatia], whose limited knowledge of Russian was evidently better than the fur traders' understanding of his Slavonic language.[12] But the Russians were pleased that the Slav read the Lord's Prayer and other prayers with them. Because of the language gap, the Spanish would bring back little information about the Russian colonies.[13] But it would

[11]Ibid., p. 29. [12]Ibid., p. 29.

[13]Khlebnikov, *Kiril, Russkaia America v neopublikovannykh zapiskakh K. T. Khlebnikova,* p. 94 (translation by Lydia Black).

be the first solid intelligence received by Viceroy of New Spain Manuel Antonio Flórez.

When López de Haro arrived at Unalaska, he found Martínez living on shore with Zaikov. The Spaniard had given the Russians ham, raisins, almonds, cheese, and wine.[14] According to López de Haro, the two commanders held long, friendly drinking bouts.[15] Zaikov gave Martínez three maps that covered the Aleutian Islands and the southern tip of Alaska. He also confirmed the alarming information that López de Haro and Narváez had picked up from Delarov. Zaikov said four Russian frigates would take possession of Nootka the following year to forestall fur trading and settlement by the English.

The British pretended to have first rights to Nootka because of Cook's discovery of the port in 1778. Natives came to the harbor to barter their fine sea otter pelts for pocket knives, fish hooks, and other items. But now the Spanish mariners were convinced the Russians were coming and might pose an even greater threat to sovereignty. The Viceroy had to be informed immediately.

Martínez may have been a skilled mariner, but he was an unpredictable commander. One day he would be friendly, alert and attentive; the next day he would turn sullen, depressed, and abusive. He insulted his subordinates and even attacked them physically during the quarrel over log records that occurred early in the voyage.[16] These temper tantrums alienated Narváez and his fellow pilots, some of whom were exiled to López de Haro's ship by the intolerant captain. The ongoing dispute

---

[14]Martínez, Estevan José, *Diario*. . . , Dec. 4, 1788.

[15]The cordiality between the Spaniards and the Russians was confirmed in 1822 by Russian historian Kiril Khlebnikov, when he met Narváez in Monterey. Khlebnikov said "Captain" Narváez recalled the expedition "with pleasure, praised the manners [behavior] of the Russians at Unalaska and said that commandant Kuzmich [Zaikov] was a very kind and fine person." (Source: Khlebnikov, op. cit., p. 94.)

[16]See fn. 30 to Narváez' journal entry for June 1, 1788.

broke out again when the two ships met at Unalaska. Martínez reviled López de Haro for collecting allegedly useless intelligence from Delarov, arrested him, and placed Narváez temporarily in command of the *San Carlos*.[17] Throughout the Alaskan expedition, the heavy-drinking Martínez allowed the *Princesa* and the *San Carlos* to get separated. On the return voyage, both ships left Unalaska August 18 and, three days later, broke off contact. López de Haro had specific instructions to meet Martínez in Monterey, California. But about 100 leagues off what is now San Francisco, he withdrew his ship from Martínez' command and, supported by Narváez and the other pilots, headed back to San Blas on his own.

The two skippers returned separately to San Blas. López de Haro arrived October 22. After waiting nearly a month in Monterey for the *San Carlos* to show up, Martínez finally set sail October 14 and reached San Blas on December 5. López de Haro had already reported the Russian plan to take over Nootka in 1789. Joined by Narváez and the other pilots, he had also lodged a strong complaint about Martínez' careless, irresponsible leadership.[18]

University of Calgary history professor Christon Archer, one of the few historians who has consistently defended, if not lauded, Martínez' conduct on this voyage, blames the "López de Haro faction" and its leader for undermining the voyage's results by provoking a near mutiny. "López de Haro prejudiced any case he might have had by neglecting his viceregal orders to examine Prince William Sound, Nootka Sound and to navigate as close to the coast as was feasible on the return voyage," argued Archer after reading Flórez' letter of November 26, 1788, to Minister of Navy Antonio Valdés.[19] "Then he

[17]See fn. 103 and 104 for Narváez' journal entries for August 4 and 5, 1788, respectively.

[18]See fn. 30 to Narváez' journal entry for June 6, 1788.

[19]Flórez to Valdés, Nov. 26, 1788, Archivo General Interior Estado, Mexico, leg. 20, ramo 34.

broke his orders from Martínez, when he decided to return to San Blas to report, rather than awaiting the *Princesa* in Monterey." Archer also claims that a visit to Nootka Sound could have alerted the Viceroy to England's activities on the Pacific Northwest coast, thereby giving Spain time to formulate a strategy to avoid the explosive confrontation that followed in 1790.[20]

Archer's first allegation is disproved by Narváez' penetration of Prince William Sound to a point well above 60°N on June 10, 1788 at López de Haro's orders. If Martínez hadn't disputed his officers' almost unanimous advice, the expedition would have gone into Prince William Sound through its eastern entrance three weeks earlier and probably reached Valdés Arm at 61°N, which remained unexplored. All of López de Haro's subsequent decisions—supported by Narváez and other pilots—were colored first by Martínez' mishandling of this initial controversy and then by his outrageous behavior at Unalaska.

Disregarding the grievances against him, Martínez immediately wrote to Viceroy Flórez in Veracruz, warning of the Russian threat on the Pacific Northwest coast. Eager to compete with Russian and British expansion, he greatly exaggerated the number of fur traders involved (Narváez estimated there were about 300 men at Unalaska and another 60 at Kodiak) and reported that the Russian navy was coming. He advised that Nootka should be occupied by a garrison early in the next year to establish Spanish possession of the coast from Nootka to San Francisco. Convinced of the northwest coast's strategic and trading importance, he offered to lead the project.

Martínez envisioned a new Spanish Pacific empire in which native people would play a significant role. His scheme

[20]Archer, Christon, "Russians, Indians & Passages," p. 138.

included a chain of Spanish missions operated by a private joint stock company, a shipbuilding industry employing native workers from Nootka to California, Spanish domination of fur trade with China, and the conquest of the Hawaiian Islands.[21]

As an unpredictable patriotic visionary and scheming rogue, Martínez was not the level-headed diplomat Spain needed to negotiate relations with either European nations or native people on America's northwest coast. His wild swings of mood, temper tantrums, drinking bouts, and abusive manners were notorious. But Flórez, who may have been Martínez' uncle, gave him the benefit of the doubt in the rift with his subordinates. Flórez dismissed López de Haro's report of the incident as being improbable. He suggested José Camacho, commandant of San Blas, investigate the allegations that Martínez had inflicted unwarranted punishment on crew members. Flórez was much more interested in the Russian threat.

In any dispute over possession rights at Nootka, the Spaniards held the whip hand with Russia, but they were acutely afraid of England. If the Russians moved in, Spain could simply withdraw privileges Russia enjoyed in Mediterranean ports. The Viceroy gave Martínez a much weaker, almost absurd argument to use with the English. Flórez instructed his captain to point out that Spanish discoveries at Nootka obviously preceded Cook's because the latter had purchased from the natives two silver tablespoons, which Martínez alleged had been stolen from him on his first expedition to the north as a pilot for Captain Juan Pérez in 1774.[22]

The Pérez expedition had anchored near the mouth of Nootka Sound but did not enter or find a suitable landing site to take formal possession for Spain. The voyagers also

[21]Archer, Christon I, "Seduction before Sovereignty," p. 21-25.

[22]Ibid., p. 21-25.

bartered there with natives, who paddled their canoes alongside the ships. But the Spaniards threw things over the side to the natives, who never came aboard. So it is unlikely that the spoons could have been stolen.[23]

To fend off challenges to Madrid's claims along the coast, Flórez instructed Martínez to build "a large hut" at Nootka and "pretend that you are engaged in settling yourself in a formal establishment." Martínez was also told to have López de Haro use the *San Carlos* to chart the coast between Nootka and Alaska and take official possession of the country. The *Princesa* and the *San Carlos* set sail February 17, 1789, commanded respectively by Martínez and López de Haro. As usual, Narváez assisted López de Haro as first pilot. Four Franciscan missionaries accompanied the expedition.

It was destined to ignite the most explosive diplomatic conflict that has ever been seen in Pacific Northwest coast history.

---

[23]Alejandro Malaspina, another important Spanish explorer, would claim later that the spoons were stolen or lost when one of Pérez' ships was attacked by Indians on the Washington coast and seven crew members were killed. If this happened, the utensils could have arrived in Nootka by trade among coastal Indians.

"VIEW OF THE ESTABLISHMENT OF THE MERCHANT SHELIKHOV ON THE ISLAND KAD'IAK,"
Engraving of Luka Voronin's drawing, 1790, in Gavriil Andreevich Sarychev's atlas to *Puteshestvie flota Kapitana Sarcheva po sieverovostochni chasti Sibiri,* St. Petersberg c. 1802. This was the original location of Grigorii I. Shelikhov's fur trading base in *Three Saints Harbor on Kodiak Island,* which was settled in 1784. The vessel is *Slava Rossjii.* Narváez was the first Spanish explorer to come ashore here.
Courtesy of Special Collections Division, University of Washington Libraries #8957.

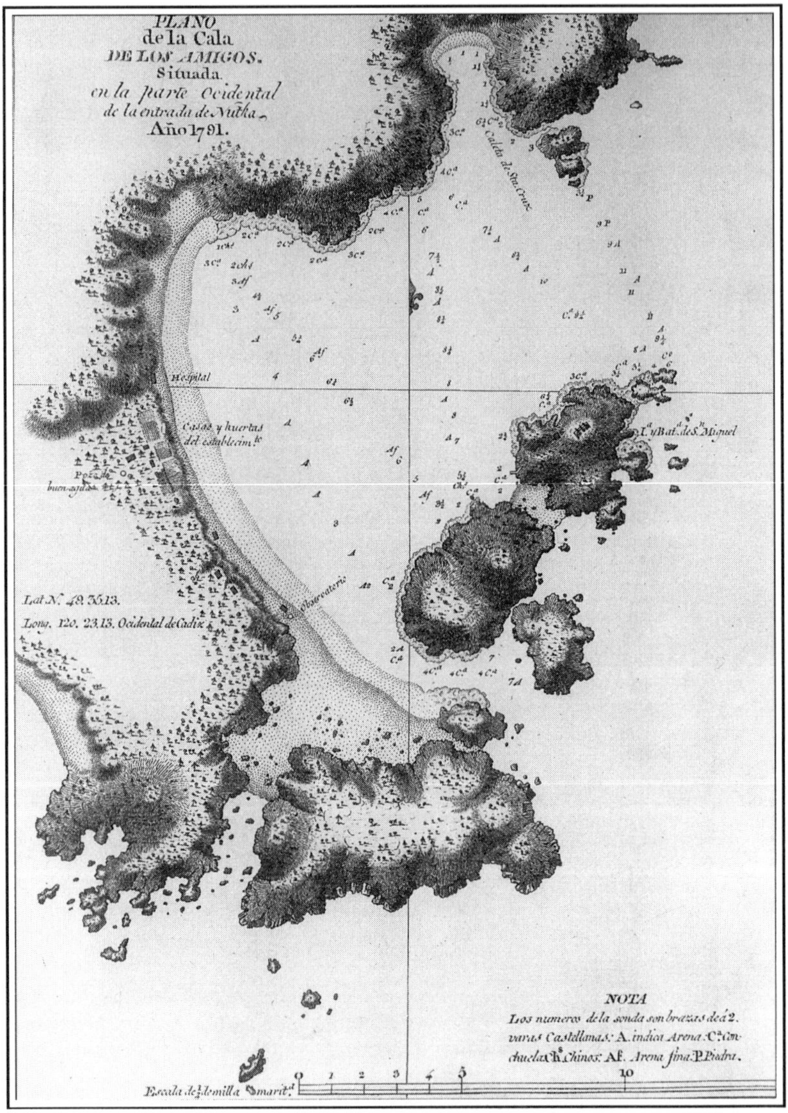

SPANISH CHART OF *CALA DE LOS AMIGOS* (FRIENDLY COVE) IN 1791. The outpost's hospital, observatory, houses, gardens and fresh water well are shown onshore. Battery guarding cove sits atop St. Michael Island. Engraved by Joseph Cardero from a drawing by Morata.
Courtesy of John Kendrick.

CHAPTER 3

Clash at Nootka, 1789-1790

Martínez arrived at Nootka May 5, 1789, to find three fur trading vessels anchored in Cala de los Amigos—two were American and one was British. Subsequently three other English merchant ships would arrive, igniting a major international dispute.

On June 8, the *Northwest America,* a 40-ton schooner commanded by Robert Funter, cruised into what the English called Friendly Cove. The small trading and coastal-exploration ship had been built there the previous summer by about 50 Chinese carpenters under the command of the English merchant-captain John Meares. Constructed around frames brought from Macao aboard the *Feliz Aventureira,* the fir-beamed, cedar-planked vessel was the first ship of European design built on the Pacific Northwest coast. As part of Martínez' effort to assert Spain's sovereignty in the port, the bellicose captain seized the *Northwest America,* claiming later that Funter had abandoned it. Two years later, Narváez would use the rebuilt, twice rechristened schooner to make his major discoveries on the northwest coast.[1]

Martínez never sent the *San Carlos* on its contemplated expedition to the north. Instead, he dispatched Narváez on June 21 in the captured schooner to investigate three major waterways to the south of Nootka Sound: the already discov-

---

[1]See Appendix A for a partial history of this vessel.

LAUNCHING OF THE *NORTHWEST AMERICA*
AT NOOTKA SOUND ON SEPTEMBER 20, 1788.
Drawing by C. Metz. This schooner was the first European-style vessel constructed on the Pacific Northwest coast. It was built by Chinese carpenters in the command of the English merchant-captain John Meares. In 1789, the Spanish captain José Martínez captured the ship from the English fur trader Robert Funter, and had it named *Santa Gertrudis la Magna.* After the vessel was modified twice, it was rechristened *Santa Saturnina,* and used by Narváez to explore Georgia Strait in 1791.
Courtesy of Vancouver Public Library, Photo #4088.

ered Clayoquot Sound, Barkley Sound and, most importantly, Juan de Fuca Strait. Martínez claimed that, returning from his first voyage to the north, he had sighted a "broad entrance" in latitude 48 degrees 20 minutes. More likely, he had picked up the information from several fur traders who had sighted the strait's entrance, but never entered. The maritime fur trade was attracting six to eight vessels a year to America's northwest coast, but their merchant captains had little interest in this waterway because they sought sea otter skins, and the animals were scarce in this vicinity. One of the merchant captains was Charles William Barkley, who gave the passage its name in 1787 but did not enter the strait.[2]

Up to 1789, Spain's only survey of the Strait was a vague, confused description made by the Greek pilot Apostolos Valerianos, serving in the Spanish Navy under the name Juan de Fuca. Legend had it that in 1592 Fuca had made a voyage in search of a northern waterway between the Atlantic and Pacific Oceans. On the northwest coast of America, he allegedly discovered a broad strait between 47 and 48 degrees of latitude north and sailed through it between lands that were "rich in gold, silver and pearls" inhabited by people clad in furs. According to the tale, Fuca reached the Atlantic Ocean after a voyage of more than 20 days.[3]

On June 24, Martínez performed an elaborate ceremony of possession. As numerous English and American merchant sailors watched, the proud Spaniard set up the customary cross, held a mass, fired salutes, and gave a flowery speech claiming all territories as far north as Alaska for King Carlos III.

After visiting the port at Nootka for several years, the English fur traders had decided to establish a settlement and sup-

---

[2]Lamb, W. Kaye, "The Mystery of Mrs. Barkley's Diary," p. 216.

[3]English engineer-historian Robert Ward has proposed a novel explanation of Apostolos Valerianos' story. Ward claims Fancis Drake "sailed into the Straight of Juan de Fuca and the Gulf of Georgia [in 1579], concluding this was the western entrance to the Northwest Passage." Ward suggests Valerianos simply passed on secret information about Drake's alleged discovery, which the Greek pilot acquired when he was captured by Thomas Cavendish, who followed Drake's route into the Pacific in 1586. After pillaging a Spanish galleon near Baja California in November 1587, Cavendish set his ship on a trans-Pacific course. But Ward says the English captain may have sent a second ship to trace Drake's course to the Northwest Passage and then back to England. That ship never returned. Documentation shows that Cavendish captured, and later released, a Greek pilot called "George." Ward says it was probably Valerianos, alias Juan de Fuca. Coincidentally, Drake had taken prisoner a pilot called "Juan Griego" at Valparaíso in 1578. Were "George" and "Juan Griego" the same person? Ward, made a fellow of the Royal Geographical Society for his research, presented his theories to the Oregon Historical Society on January 25, 1996. (See Bawlf, Sam, "Drake beat Cook and the rest . . . ," p. A-17.)

ply base there. To this end, Captain James Colnett was the next Britisher to sail into Nootka. After a drunken brawl with the assertive, insolent Englishman, the equally churlish Martínez commandeered both Colnett's ship, the *Argonaut,* and a 43-foot sloop under his command called the *Princess Royal,* which had arrived a few days earlier. Then he arrested the crews, including 29 Chinese craftsmen, and placed Colnett in chains. The Spaniard's impulsive belligerence set off a clash between the rival nations that would take almost eighteen months to settle.

Forcing the captured Chinese to work, Martínez built a small battery on an islet that commanded the entrance to Friendly Cove, erected a few sheds, and started constructing a large building on the main beach. Except for their commander, he allowed the British "prisoners" to do what they wanted. Colnett remained confined. But on July 4, when the two American captains invited all officers in the Cove to join them in honoring the United States, Colnett was released for the celebration. He would eventually suffer a mental breakdown and attempt suicide.

Meanwhile, Narváez had been exploring the three large waterways to the south. Having penetrated Juan de Fuca Strait for more than 25 leagues, Narváez returned to Nootka July 5 with Spain's first precise descriptions of the waterway on which Martínez placed great importance. Others had previously found and probed the strait's entrance,[4] but Narváez was the first European to chart its interior. Today, the international boundary between Canada and the United States fol-

[4]In August 1788, the Englishman Charles Duncan anchored just inside the entrance near Cape Flattery. His sketch of the opening was published in early 1790, with a note stating the natives called the waterway a "great sea." During the summer of 1788, the English fur trader John Meares reached the strait and sent his longboat eleven leagues inside. In March 1789, the American Robert Gray sailed into the strait for 25 miles before foul weather forced him back. He reported that "a large sea" opened to the east. In May 1789, they concluded that they had discovered, in what is now Dixon Entrance, the Northwest Passage. (See: Williams, Glyndwr, "Myth and Reality ...," pp. 3-5.)

lows the center line of this important waterway. Narváez told Martínez:

> From side to side it measured 21 miles, continued on inland for almost the same width as far as one could see, no horizon being visible in the east-southeast, and is the strait which they call Juan de Fuca. Inside is a port named San Juan [Port Renfrew] which is a good place to anchor in, to take water and wood and to provide oneself with timber for planks and masts. It is at the farthest north and west point.[5]

Martínez was convinced the strait led to the fabled Northwest Passage, sought by maritime explorers for decades. He believed it might connect to either the Mississippi River or the legendary Strait of Fonte in the area of Hudson Bay. He was confident confirmation of its exact location would startle everyone in Europe. In his opinion, it had to be explored further.

First he had to deal with another English fur trader who sailed into Nootka Sound aboard the *Princess Royal*. This captain, seeking Colnett, tried to contact Martínez through the natives at Nootka. The wily Spaniard lured the English vessel into Friendly Cove, captured it, and took the captain and crew prisoners of war. Martínez was on board the ship July 13, when Chief Callicum, the son-in-law of Chief Maquinna and one of the most respected warriors among the Mowachahts, came alongside in a canoe, shouting accusations about Martínez being a thief. Infuriated by the insults, Martínez grabbed a musket, drew a bead on the abusive chief, and pulled the trigger. But the gun misfired. A Spanish sailor fired

---

[5]Martínez, Estevan José, *Diario...*, July 5, 1789, as translated by Wagner in *Spanish Explorations...*, p. 4; *A translation of the Diary of Estevan José Martínez...* in *The Journal of Captain James Colnett....* According to Martínez, Narváez also described his visit to "a very fine port named by the native Indians 'Clayocuat' [Clayoquot Sound] and by our people 'Puerto de Narváez.'" Narváez found "populous settlements in the port, all under the command of a king or chief, Huicananish [Wickininish]." He visited the Indians and found them "friendly," "addicted to trade" and "accustomed to carry on war with those to the south." He said they considered the Nootka superior warriors.

MAQUINNA, PRINCIPAL CHIEF AT NOOTKA IN 1791.
The design woven into his cedar bark hat advertises his skill at hunting killer whales. The finial on top identifies him as a chief. This engraving was made from a drawing by Tomás de Suría circa 1788. *Courtesy of John Kendrick.*

another gun, killing Callicum on the spot. It remained unclear whether the chief was accusing Martínez of stealing the ships or misappropriating lumber from the Nootkans. But the natives remembered the incident with bitterness for years.

On July 27, Martínez placed López de Haro and Narváez in command of the *San Carlos* and the captured *Princess Royal* respectively, and sent them back to San Blas with the news about discovering the entrance to the Northwest Passage. Both ships reached their home port by the end of August. Meanwhile, Viceroy Flórez had dispatched another ship to Nootka with orders for Martínez to end the "pretended" settlement before winter set in. To house his prisoners, Martínez had been building a jail aboard another captured ship. He completely evacuated Nootka October 31 and set sail for San Blas with his prisoners and captured ships. (The vessels included the former *Northwest America,* reconditioned and renamed *Santa Gertrudis la Magna.*) Martínez' departure placed Spain's claim to the surrounding area in serious jeopardy.

Flórez knew that Martínez' fight with Colnett would stir up trouble with England, but the Viceroy had already resigned, so he simply filed a full report with Madrid and waited for his successor's arrival. Unfortunately, Flórez' dispatch failed to mention his latest order to Martínez, recalling him to San Blas.

The diplomatic firestorm set off by Martínez' reckless performance at Nootka would be dumped in the lap of a new administration—one that was even more determined to secure Spain's position on the Pacific Northwest coast.

RETURN TO NOOTKA—In mid-August of 1789, Viceroy Juan Vicente de Guemes Pacheco de Padilla Horcacitas y Aguayo, Count Revilla Gigedo, landed in Veracruz with seven top-flight naval officers and four surgeons assigned to the Pacific Northwest coast. The assignments showed Madrid's commitment to occupying Nootka as Flórez had urged. The senior naval officer was Juan Francisco Bodega y Quadra, who would serve as commandant at San Blas until his death in 1794. His genial, diplomatic style made him the ideal man to take charge of the delicate developments taking place at Nootka. The calm, conciliatory commander spearheaded Spain's intensive exploration of the northwest coast, which picked up steam in 1790. It would give Narváez many opportunities to use his navigation and cartographic skills.

Revilla Gigedo would emerge as one of the greatest viceroys to govern Mexico. On October 17, 1789, he took over from Flórez and faced two major questions: What to do about the captured Englishmen and their vessels in San Blas? How to hang on to Nootka? Giving the second challenge priority, he wrote Bodega in early December, instructing him to "relieve Martínez" and replace him with an officer "who might be more worthy of confidence" to occupy and fortify Nootka and explore inside Juan de Fuca Strait. He said

ESTEBAN JOSÉ MARTÍNEZ (1742–1798) (left) and JUAN FRANCISCO DE LA BODEGA Y QUADRA (1744–1794) (right). Martínez was an experienced captain who became convinced Russians posed a threat on Pacific Northwest coast. His arrest of English fur traders sparked the "Nootka crisis." Bodega y Quadra was commandant of San Blas naval base in Mexico, which supplied Spain's California presidios, its Nootka outpost, and exploration of the Pacific Northwest coast. *Courtesy of Museo Naval, Madrid (left) and and oil by Julio Garcia Condoy, c. 1950, Maritime Museum, Victoria (right).*

Martínez' notion of a "northwest passage" belonged to "the same sphere of dreams" as other mythological voyages.

To Bodega's consternation, Martínez arrived in San Blas on December 6, only a few days after the Viceroy's letter was delivered. Bodega decided to make Martínez the scapegoat for evacuating Nootka. Two days before Christmas, Bodega answered Gigedo saying: "The total state of abandonment in which Martínez left Nootka and the necessity of keeping possession of it are today the principal objects of my attention." Bodega gathered all the artillery he could find and loaded it aboard the frigate *Concepción,* the *San Carlos,* and the renamed English sloop, *Princesa Real.* Bodega appointed Lieutenant Francisco Eliza commandant of Nootka and ordered Salvador Fidalgo and Manuel Quimper to accompany him. Reluctantly, he agreed to send Martínez along as an unranked special officer with absolutely no responsibility.

The first item in Bodega's secret instructions to Eliza stated that the expedition's primary objective was to fortify Nootka before some other power took over. But Bodega also said "the King requires that you do not molest the English . . . nor prevent them by force from establishing themselves in the neighborhood." Next, he was to explore the entire coast, including Juan de Fuca Strait. As soon as Eliza returned to Nootka he was to send a vessel straight to San Blas with plans and details, including careful records of the 6,000 pounds of large copper sheets, measuring 26 inches by 22 inches and "thick as a real," which he carried to trade for furs.

Commanding the *Concepción,* Eliza sailed from San Blas on February 3, 1790, in charge of the largest Spanish force sent northward up to that time. He was accompanied by the *San Carlos,* with Fidalgo in charge, and the sloop *Princesa Real,* skippered by Quimper. On April 4, the expedition would be reinforced by two more frigates—the *Princesa,* carrying Narváez as pilot under the command of Lieutenant Jacinto Caamaño, and the *Aranzazu,* commanded by Juan Bautista Matute.

Fortunately, when Eliza arrived at Nootka April 4, Friendly Cove was still unoccupied by either English or Russians. The natives, who considered the sheltered bay a favored campsite which they called Yuquot, pulled up stakes and moved. They had been alienated by Martínez' killing of Chief Callicum. During the next two years of occupation, the natives continually asked the Spaniards when they planned to leave.

Veteran first pilot Juan Pantoja found the natives "docile and cowardly" compared with the more warlike aborigines farther south. He said they lived in board-roofed post-and-beam longhouses. The men wore "pine bark" capes over calf-length under garments. The women wrapped themselves in a breech cloth. Pantoja reported that the natives enslaved enemies taken in war and that the chiefs occasionally ate some of the youngest captives. "Fifteen Indians of both sexes from four to ten years of age have been obtained in exchange for copper and [abalone] shells," said Pantoja. "The principal land and sea officers undertook to raise and educate them."[6]

Pantoja also reported that poor diets and the long, wet northwest winters left the Spaniards suffering colds, colic, rheumatism, scurvy, and diarrhea or bloody dysentery. "The last two are very common and almost incurable in this climate," he said.

At the end of May, Eliza sent out two expeditions. Fidalgo and first pilot Estevan Mondofía sailed aboard the *San Carlos* to explore the Alaska coast. Quimper left on the *Princesa Real* with first pilot López de Haro and second pilot Carrasco to chart both interior coasts of Juan de Fuca Strait as far as the San Juan Islands. With this work completed, Quimper was forced to sail south, arriving in San Blas November 13. Fidalgo also returned to Mexico.

Left at Nootka, Eliza would not find out what his officers had discovered until the following spring. Meanwhile, Caamaño had sailed the *Aranzazu* into Nootka in late June with Narváez on board. Eliza had already started constructing several buildings on shore. He immediately transferred Narváez to the depot-guardship *Concepción.* Narváez would remain under Eliza's command for the next two years, as the Spanish commander did his best to impede the English from taking possession of this important outpost.[7] It was the only non-

[6]Pantoja y Arriaga, Juan, *Extracto de la navegación . . . 1791,* (translated in Wagner, *Spanish Explorations...,* pp. 161-62).

[7]Marina de Guerra, *Estado de los méritos y servicios del Primer Piloto . . . Don José María Narváez,* p.3.

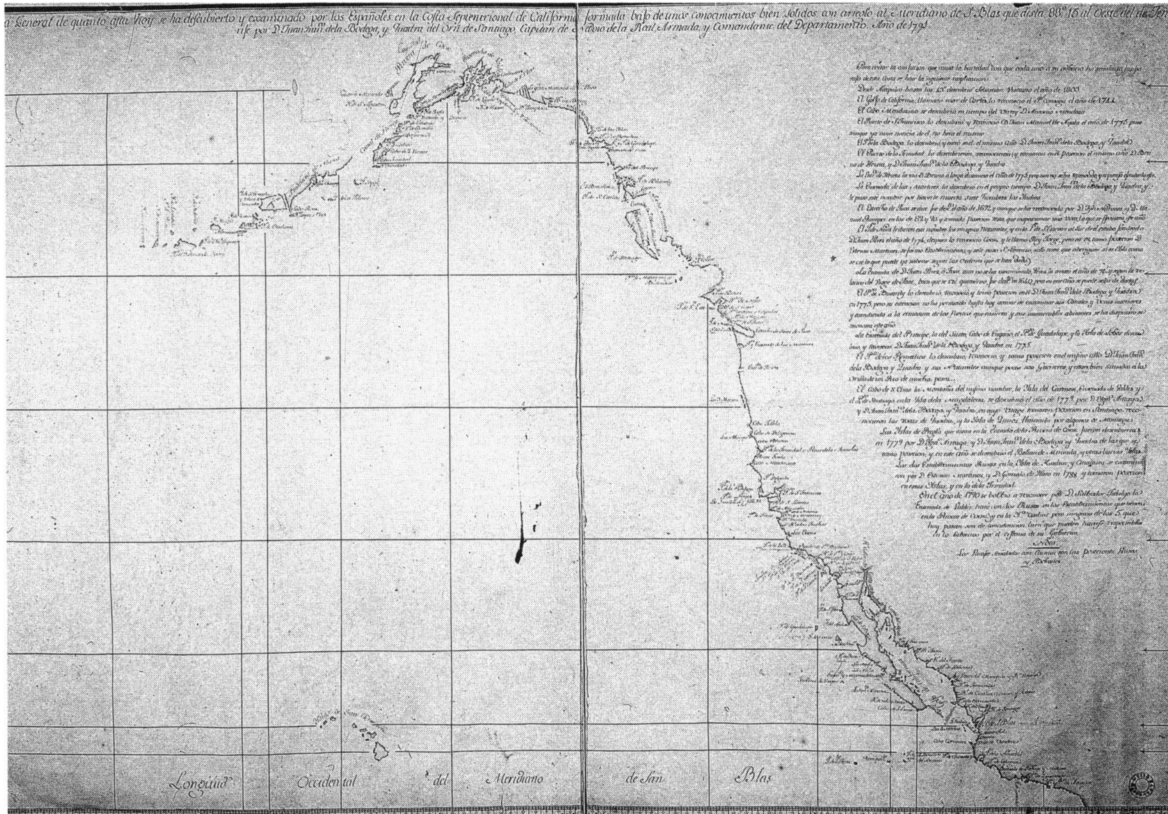

JUAN FRANCISCO DE LA BODEGA Y QUADRA'S *CARTA GENERAL . . .* OF 1791.
Summarizing Spanish exploration and discovery on the coast of the Californias and northward, it shows the old Spanish place names from Puerto de Acapulco to the Aleutian Islands. Bodega made the chart at San Blas in 1791, where he had been appointed commandante, and sent it to Madrid with notes of explanation. In them he states that, although the Strait of Juan de Fuca was "surveyed and taken possession of in 1789 and 1790 by Don Jose de Narváez and Don Manuel Quimper [respectively], yet one mouth has not yet been inspected, but it is purposed to do so this year [1791]. *Courtesy of Museo Naval.*

native establishment between San Francisco and Prince William Sound.

Martínez' seizures of English ships had enraged the British public, sparking the famous Nootka Sound controversy. British negotiators sought to secure undisputed fur-trading rights in the north Pacific. Spain clung to its time-worn theory that she possessed complete sovereignty in the South Sea, given to her by Pope Alexander VI in 1493 when he divided the New World between Spain and Portugal. Spain feared that settlements in the Pacific Northwest by heavily armed British fur-trading vessels would endanger her possessions in California. When Britain threatened to declare war over the controversy, Spain decided to sign the Nootka Convention October 28, 1790, effectively abandoning its claim of exclusive sovereignty. The Convention left ownership of the region unsettled and gave Britain and Spain equal trading rights.

Meanwhile, explorers of all the nations that had economic, political, and military interest in the Pacific Northwest coast continued to search for a Northwest Passage—that elusive arctic link between the Atlantic and Pacific Oceans. One of them was Narváez.

CHAPTER 4

In Quest of the Passage

In 1609, Captain Lorenzo Ferrer de Maldonado, a respected navigator from Madrid, presented a long report to the king describing a remarkable voyage he pretended to have made in 1588. Ferrer claimed he had sailed from east to west through the Strait of Anian, crossing the North American continent at about sixty degrees North latitude. His proposed scheme for securing control of the imaginary passage came to naught. But the illusion persisted.

Two Frenchmen—cartographer Nicolas Delisle and geographer Philippe Buache—became dazzled by the novelty and importance of this hoax when they came across a remarkable letter that had been published in 1708. The writer was Bartolome Fonte, a Spanish admiral who claimed he had explored the Strait of Anian for the viceroy in 1640. It was another fake. But Delisle and Buache became convinced of its authenticity and presented it as a true document to the Académie des Sciences in Paris in 1750. Buache said this was indeed the long-sought route between the Pacific and Atlantic oceans. Two years later, the Frenchmen published an imaginary map, which retained its credibility for more than forty years.[1]

On November 13, 1790, cartographer Jean-Nicolas

[1] Mathes, Michael W., "The Province of Anian and its Strait," p. 19.

Buache de la Neuville, nephew of Philippe Buache, reignited the controversy when he read a memorial before the Académie des Sciences, defending the existence of the imaginary passage and endorsing the credibility of the recently revived manuscript describing Ferrer's trip through the "Strait of Anian."[2]

To test Buache de la Neuville's opinions, Spain would order the corvettes *Descubierta* and *Atrevida*—commissioned for a scientific voyage around the world and harbored in Acapulco—to survey Juan de Fuca Strait. With Alejandro Malaspina in command, the two ships would eventually sail north from Acapulco on May 1, 1791. On June 23, Malaspina would verify earlier surveys by Captain Cook, but he would not enter the strait.

Meanwhile, Bodega was organizing another probe of the waters beyond Juan de Fuca Strait. In February 1791, Ensign Ramón Saavedra left San Blas in command of the storeship *San Carlos* and sailed for Nootka, with pilot Juan Pantoja aboard. He carried much needed supplies and Viceroy Revilla Gigedo's new instructions for Eliza, which were based on Quimper's discoveries. Eliza was to finish the survey that was arousing the curiosity of geographers, by extending exploration into the uncharted waters of what is now Georgia Strait. The *San Carlos* arrived at Nootka on March 26.

These orders were modified in late June, when the frigate *Aranzazu* arrived from San Blas with a supplementary letter from Bodega related to the recently completed Nootka Convention. Bodega also enclosed a general plan of the coast, which summarized Spanish discoveries between Acapulco and the Aleutian Islands up to 1791. Bodega had finished the *Carta General* in San Blas in March and sent the original to Madrid. The chart indicates that the large inland sea which

[2]Inglis, Robin, *Spain and the North Pacific Coast*, pp. 58, 119, 184; Wagner, Henry, *Spanish Voyages...*, p. CXII.

YUQUOT (FRIENDLY COVE) ON AUGUST 12, 1791, WHEN MALASPINA EXPEDITION ARRIVED.

Working from a Felipe Bauzá sketch (*Playa y establecimiento de Nutka,* Museo Naval), Fernando Brambila made this more elaborate drawing in either Mexico or Madrid. The commandant's house is on shore behind the depot-guardship *Concepción*, moored at Nootka two years and not in use in 1791. The second ship is an unidentified British trader, probably the brigantine *Venus,* commanded by William Hervey. As no observatory (finished Aug. 13) can be seen on shore, Bauzá's sketch was one of the first made by Malaspina's artists. It is the same as Brambila's "improved" drawing, but it has no ships or boats in the bay and the trees are drawn less accurately. Brambila never went north of Acapulco. *Courtesy of Museo de América.*

SPANISH FLAG FLIES FROM BATTERY GUARDING ENTRANCE TO YUQUOT (FRIENDLY COVE) IN 1791.

The *Concepción's* decks were covered and upper masts and rigging lowered while Eliza led an expedition into the Gran Canal aboard the *San Carlos.* Behind the tallest mast is the expedition's observatory on shore. This engraving, from a drawing by Fernando Brambila who "improved" on a sketch by José Cardero, was made for the 1802 publication of the *Relación* of the Galiano/Valdés voyage of 1792. *Courtesy of Museo Naval.*

runs north from Juan de Fuca Strait remained unexplored. One of Bodega's notes on the chart states: "El Estrecho de Fuca, it is said, was discovered in 1592; and although surveyed and taken possession of in 1789 and 1790 by Don José Maria Narváez and Don Manuel Quimper [respectively], yet one mouth has not yet been inspected, but it is purposed to do so this year."

The special expedition that Eliza was instructed to command would lead to Narváez' major discoveries in the Pacific Northwest. Eliza eventually received most of the credit for the expedition, but he actually did no exploring himself throughout the entire voyage.

On May 3, the expeditionary force placed the statue of their patron saint, the Virgin of Rosario in the carpenter shop at Nootka, decorated it with flags and flowers and held a special Mass. Firing rifles and shouting *"Viva la Virgen,"* the crew boarded their vessels. The next day, Eliza placed Saavedra in charge of guarding Nootka with about 85 sailors and 31 soldiers under Captain Pedro Alberni. Most of the rank and file were Mexican.[3] Sailing out of the harbor in command of the *San Carlos,* which was 72-feet-long (at the keel), Eliza headed north for three days. Then he realized his orders to make a detailed map of the entire coast between Bucareli Bay (now in Alaska) and Puerto de la Trinidad (north of San Francisco) were unrealistic. Reversing his course, he wisely decided to concentrate on Juan de Fuca Strait.

Juan Pantoja and José Antonio Verdía served as Eliza's first and second pilots respectively. Verdía had apprenticed under Narváez on Martínez' expeditions to Alaska in 1788 and to Nootka in 1789. Their lead ship had a 22-foot beam, a 15-foot draft, and it carried 16 four-pound cannons. Aboard the larger vessel were surgeon Juan Teron and chaplain José Joaquin Villaverde. The packetship also carried a longboat.

[3]Inglis, op. cit., p. 85.

The *San Carlos* was accompanied by the schooner *Santa Saturnina,* which was 32-feet-10-inches long on the keel with an 11-foot-10-inch beam.[4] She had been reassembled in Nootka from the dismantled *Santa Gertrudis la Magna,* which Bodega had ordered returned. Nicknamed *La Orcasitas,* the schooner was skippered by Narváez and piloted by Juan Carrasco, who would make the most complete chart of the expedition. The shallow (five-foot draft) schooner was outfitted with eight two-man oars and armed with four three-pound cannons on deck. She carried about 20-days' supply of food for both her crew and the longboat's small expeditionary force. The 28-foot longboat had thirteen oars but little space for storing provisions.

On May 7, both ships anchored in Clayoquot Sound, the first major inlet south of Nootka on Vancouver Island's west coast. Two days later, Narváez and Carrasco set off to explore the interior of this waterway. Returning on the 14th, they spent seven days collaborating on a chart of what they called Puerto Clayucuat.[5] (It would appear later as an inset on Carrasco's chart of the entire voyage.)

Meanwhile, Pantoja investigated the sound's outer reaches and Eliza made friends with the powerful Chief Wickaninish. "In a dance of young men which Guicananich gave me in his house, more than 600 took part," wrote Eliza. He said the Indians had five large settlements, each of which was occupied by about 1,500 people. He said the largest was Guicananich (Wickininish) with 2,500 inhabitants.[6]

From May 21 to June 10, Narváez and Carrasco also charted Puerto de Boca Carrasco (Barkley Sound), while Eliza sailed south to the entrance of Juan de Fuca Strait.[7] Narváez

[4]See Appendix B.

[5]Carrasco, Juan, *Extract of the voyage... 1791,* as translated by Wagner in *Spanish Explorations...*, p. 200.

[6]Eliza, Francisco, *Extract of the voyage...*, Nootka, October 10, 1791, as translated by Wagner in op. cit., pp.145, 146.

[7]Carrasco, op. cit., as translated by Wagner in op. cit., p. 200.

The Spanish schooner *Santa Saturnina* under command of Second Pilot José Narváez sailing in Georgia Strait off Grant Island about July 12, 1791 after leaving anchorage on west side of Isla San Ignacio (Thormanby Island).
Oil by Steve Mayo, 1980.

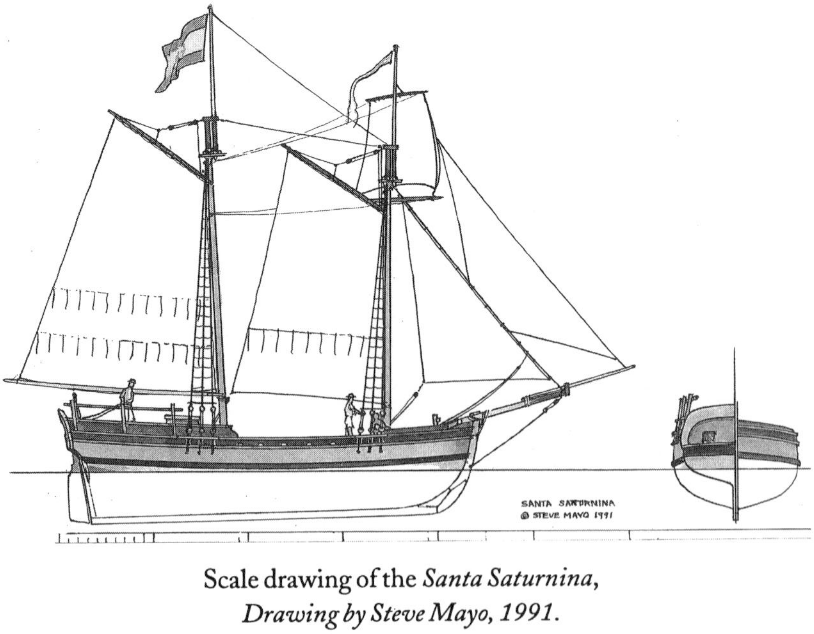

Scale drawing of the *Santa Saturnina*,
Drawing by Steve Mayo, 1991.

had told the commander "he was the only one who had been there in the year 1789" and he knew the larger ship could neither enter the sound nor find sufficient shelter.[8]

After finding all these inlets "closed," both ships rendezvoused at Cordova (Esquimalt) on June 11. According to Eliza's summary of the voyage, Narváez reported that the Boca de Carrasco (Barkley Sound) was a "large archipelago of islands" in which "he had seen five large settlements" of "warlike and daring" Indians. "On two occasions" 200 natives attacked Narváez, "but he held them in check by means of some cannon shot." He said the natives "were surprised to see the schooner and, according to their explanations, had never seen a vessel inside."[9]

From June 14 to 24, Pantoja took command of the schooner and longboat and explored the southern Gulf Islands, assisted by Narváez, Carrasco and Verdía. Sailing north in the Canal de López de Aro (Haro Strait), Pantoja reached the north end of Isla de Sallas (the two Pender Islands

[8] Eliza, op. cit., as translated by Wagner in op. cit., p. 146.
[9] Ibid, p. 149.

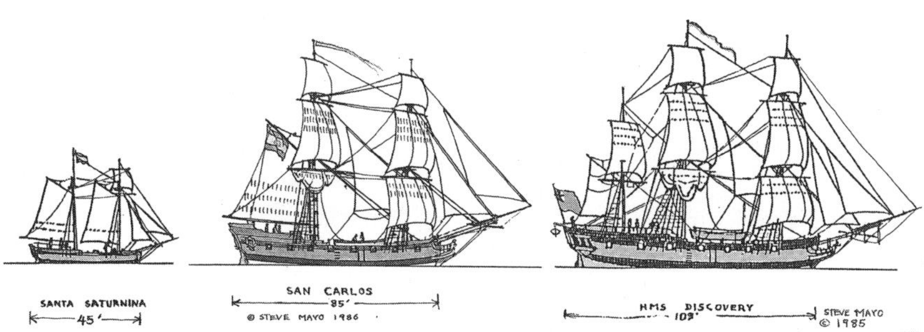

Comparison of Narváez' and Vancouver's vessels,
Drawings by Steve Mayo.

called Isla San Euevio by Carrasco), where he realized there were several openings to the west, which he named Bocas de Bazan. He also concluded there were two passes to the east and decided to investigate the larger, southeastern arm (Boundary Pass) the next day.

"The 15th dawned clear with a light wind from the east," wrote Pantoja. "At three in the morning we weighed anchor." Three hours later he anchored in Puerto de San Antonio (Bedwell Harbor). Towing the schooner with the longboat, Pantoja crossed the mouth of Plumper Sound, which he explored until 3:00 P.M. At seven in the evening Pantoja's exhausted crew rowed both ships around the east end of Saturna Island, where he saw "a grand and extended canal," which he named El Gran Canal de Nuestra Senora del Rosario la Marinera (Georgia Strait) "in honor of our patroness as it was the most important place we had discovered up to the present." He recorded sighting "a small hill like a sugar loaf" (Lasqueti Island) on the horizon to the north and "very high mountains covered with snow" (the Cascades) to the east. The Spaniards believed they had found the long-sought inland sea. They were convinced it would lead to a passage eastward to Hudson Bay or the Mississippi River.[10]

That night Pantoja anchored at tiny Patos Island in the eastern entrance to Boundary Pass. The next day he searched in vain for an eastern channel to the south. "We found ourselves in another great archipelago," he wrote. Two days overdue, running out of food, his men exhausted from rowing, Pantoja turned back. Rowing out of Haro Strait against the wind, the longboat's crew reached Cordova June 24.

Narváez returned the next day in the *Santa Saturnina*. The young navigator was about to set off on what would prove to be his most significant voyage of exploration.

---

[10]Pantoja, Juan, *Extract of the navigation...*, as translated by Wagner in op. cit., p. 174-76.

NARVÁEZ IN GEORGIA STRAIT, 1791—At the port of Cordova, Eliza and his three master pilots immediately planned a major exploration of the Gran Canal. The commander proposed taking the *San Carlos* inside so she could keep the expedition supplied. But the pilots convinced him the packetboat risked shipwreck in the complex, uncharted waters. Eliza also fell sick. To get closer to their task, the officers agreed to move their base to Puerto de Quadra (Port Discovery) on the south side of Juan de Fuca Strait. The entire expedition anchored there June 28.

On July 1, 1791, Narváez set sail in the same exploration vessels used by Pantoja and presumably with the same crew: 30 Mexican sailors and eight Spanish soldiers (Carrasco's log says there were five). According to senior pilot Pantoja, he remained at Quadra with Eliza "as there was no other officer of war to assist the chief."

With Carrasco as pilot on the tiny schooner and Verdía as brevet pilot aboard the longboat, Narváez passed through Rosario Strait (which he renamed Canal de Fidalgo), east of what are now called the San Juan Islands. He surveyed Islas de Guemes (Guemes Island), San Vincente (Cypress Island), and Pacheco (Lummi Island). The 41-member expedition also visited Seno Padillo (Padilla Bay), anchored in Puerto Socorro (Chukanut Bay) and passed Seno Gaston (Bellingham Bay). Heading north into the Gran Canal, Narváez continued charting those parts of the strait's eastern shore that he could see. Shoals and adverse winds often forced the ships offshore; fog and rain sometimes hid the land.

Narváez' next anchorages were Puerto del Garzon (Birch Bay) and Punta de San José (Drayton Harbor). Passing Punta de San Rafael (Ocean Park), Narváez cruised around the shores of Boca de Bodega (Boundary Bay). The latter was changed on Carrasco's chart to Boca de Floridablanca, the last name of Spain's prime minister. Here Narváez formed the strange impression that the inland sea extended far to the northeast, possibly reaching what is now Burrard Inlet.

One researcher[11] has concluded that the Fraser River may have flooded a large part of its delta, creating the impression of a huge expanse of water. Eleven months later, another Spanish expedition led by Dionisio Alcala Galiano used Narváez' findings to search for the large *boca* (mouth) on his sketch. But the explorers only found a huge land mass blocking the way. Their reaction to the discovery, so contradictory to what Carrasco's chart had suggested, is reflected in the name they gave to the area: Bahía del Eñgano or Ensenada del Eñgano (Deception Bay).

The explorers also rounded Islas de Zepeda (Point Roberts), which they thought was an island. From there Narváez sailed about two leagues along the shore through "a line of white water [that was] more sweet than salt."[12] Failing to realize he was passing mouths of the great Fraser River at freshet, Narváez sighted openings between what he assumed were low-lying islands. Continuing northward, Narváez anchored off a headland, later called Point Grey. He assumed it was one of three islands in the area—(marked Isla(s) de Langara on Carrasco's chart). The other two must have been Sea and Iona Islands.

From their village to the southeast, large numbers of Musqueam Indians paddled out to the schooner in slim dugout canoes.[13] At first the explorers were alarmed until they realized the natives did not carry bows and arrows. They brought several kinds of fish, including large freshly caught salmon. The natives traded deer and elk meat, native vegetables, water and firewood for scraps of copper, pieces of iron,

[11]Bartroli, Tomas, *Discovery of the Site of Vancouver City by José María Narváez in 1791*, p. 17.

[12]Pantoja, op. cit., as translated by Wagner in op. cit., p. 186.

[13]Eliza, op. cit., as translated by Wagner in op. cit., p. 152.

MUSQUEAM CHIEF DRAWN BY JOSÉ CARDERO ON GALIANO-VALDÉS EXPEDITION IN 1792. His people met Narváez in 1791 off Point Grey (Punta de Langara). *Courtesy of Museo Naval.*

and barrel hoops. The Spaniards noticed that the Musqueam language was different from that of the Nootkas. Using sign language, the Musqueams made it clear that the canal continued much farther on. The natives also managed to explain that ships much larger than the *Santa Saturnina* had sailed earlier somewhere in the Gran Canal, (probably in Juan de Fuca Strait), and that one of them carried brass bracelets engraved with knives.

Narváez' store-keeper, José Ignacio Gonzalez, bought an eleven-year-old native boy. From the youngster, the Spaniards learned that many Indians came on horseback from "flat country" in the northeast to trade iron, copper and blue beads for fish. Their visits lasted two months.[14]

There is no record of the Spaniards going ashore to visit the Musqueam village. But they did explore the shore (near Point Grey) in the longboat, collecting some drinkable water from

[14]Pantoja, op. cit., as translated by Wagner in op. cit., p. 187.

the sea's surface and concluding that it came from a "very copious" river—undoubtedly the north arm of the large Fraser River. Foul weather kept them from locating it precisely.[15]

Another native settlement is located on Carrasco's chart at Punta de la Bodega (Point Atkinson) so we can be sure that the voyagers observed the shores of today's North and West Vancouver, where the Squamish Indians camped in large numbers. A third village is indicated on the pointed headland at the entrance to Bocas del Carmelo (Howe Sound), which Narváez charted next along with the Islas de Apodaca (Bowen Island and nearby islets). Instead of entering this large sound, Narváez sailed northwest along the coast and anchored at a watering place named Rio de la Aguada (probably Wilson Creek), directly opposite what are now called the White Islets. This is the only documentary evidence of the explorers going ashore anywhere near what is now Greater Vancouver.

From his next anchorage off Isla de San Ignacio (Thormanby Island), Narváez sailed between Islas de San Felix (Texada Island) and the mainland. As the feast of San Felix is held on July 12, we can assume that was the date on which he reached this location. He gave the name Isla de Texada to what is now called Lasqueti Island. But the expedition was running low on rations.

Reaching a point about opposite the south end of Hardy Island, some 40 to 50 leagues from Puerto de Quadra and at the latitude of Nootka Sound, Narváez turned back. Rounding Lasqueti Island, he sailed north again a short distance, sighting Punta de Laso de la Vega (Cape Lazo) to the west on Vancouver Island. In the distance to the north, he apparently spotted the high lands at the head of the gulf: Campo Alange (Quadra Island north of Cape Mudge) and the unidentifiable Punta de San Luis, which were separated by Boca de Flórez (Sutil Channel).

[15]Eliza, op. cit., as translated by Wagner in op. cit., pp. 151-52.

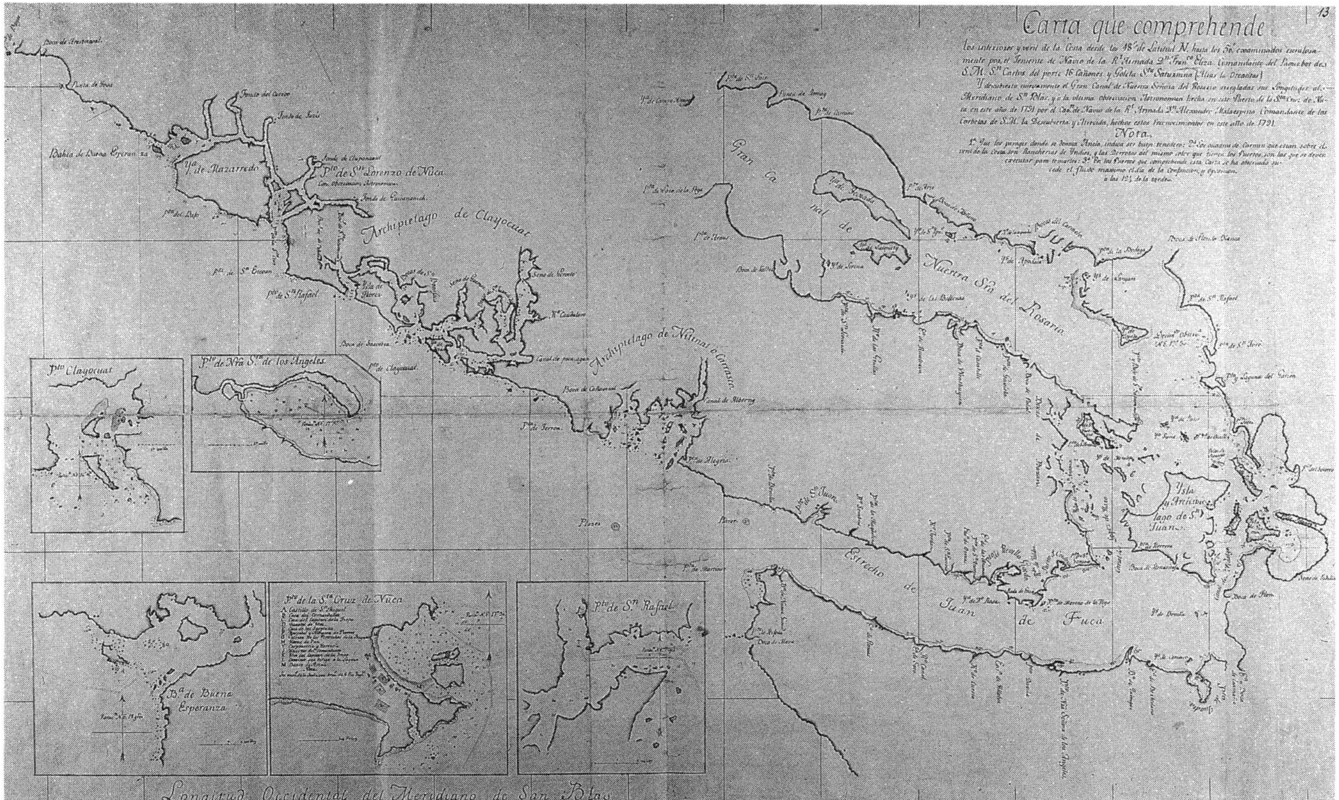

The original "Carta que comprehende . . ." drawn by Juan Carrasco in 1791 and often mistakenly referred to as the "Narváez Chart." It summarizes discoveries made by Carrasco, Pantoja, and Narváez during Eliza's stay in the Strait of Juan de Fuca. Located in Deposito Hydrografico, Madrid. *Courtesy of Museo Naval.*

Heading southwest across the Gran Canal, Narváez rounded Isla de Lerena (Hornby Island) and followed the Vancouver Island coast southward. En route, he explored various passages and ports, including Bocas de Winthuysen (the site of Nanaimo, named by Carrasco after Francisco Javier Winthuysen, head of the Naval College in Madrid). The presence of numerous large whales in the Gran Canal caused Narváez to speculate that they had entered by some other route than Juan de Fuca Strait. At Boca de Porlier (Porlier Pass) between Valdés and Galiano Islands, he headed southeast across the Gran Canal and passed through Rosario Strait. On July 22, the expedition returned to Puerto de Quadra. Narváez' supplies were exhausted.

When Narváez had departed on the three-week expedition, he had noticed a large entrance in the Ensenada de Caamaño (Admiralty Inlet). As it was only about seven miles from Puerto de Quadra, he planned to explore it on his return. But he ran out of food at the end of the voyage and Eliza was eager to sail back to Nootka and send his report to San Blas. If the commander hadn't given up his plan to accompany Narváez' exploration with the *San Carlos,* he could have kept the smaller vessels supplied, and supported a longer expedition into Puget Sound to the south and through the Inside Passage to the north.

The Spaniards missed a golden opportunity to make both discoveries one year before Captain George Vancouver sailed these waters. But Spain finally had its first picture of the size and shape of the inland sea that so many European navigators had sought.

CHAPTER 5

Spanish Influence Wanes

On July 26, 1791, the packetship *San Carlos* and the schooner *Santa Saturnina* left Puerto de Quadra and headed west in Juan de Fuca Strait, toward the open sea. Carrasco was given command of the schooner because Eliza needed Narváez to help draw charts and draft the report to Bodega. Beating their way north along the outer coast of Vancouver Island, the ships encountered heavy northwest winds. During the night of August 14, the two crews lost sight of each other.

The *San Carlos* pressed on and managed to reach Nootka August 30. Eliza was surprised to learn that, in his absence, the great scientific expedition headed by Alejandro Malaspina had visited the Pacific Northwest coast, stopped at Nootka, and left for Monterey, California the previous day. Eliza would have to wait four months to report Narváez' discoveries, which he considered remarkable.

But Carrasco would deliver the latest news about what was still thought to be the Northwest Passage much sooner. After losing sight of the *San Carlos,* he battled stiff headwinds round the clock for fourteen days. Low on provisions and water, he was forced to sail south, arriving at Monterey September 15.[1]

---

[1]Carrasco, Juan, *Extract of the voyage . . . 1791,* as translated by Wagner in *Spanish Explorations. . .* , p. 201. Malaspina says Carrasco arrived on the 16th: Malaspina, Alejandro, *Viaje politico-cientifico . . . 1789-1794,* Vol. 1, Book 2, pp. 291-92. For more on the exact date see: Cutter, Donald C., *Malaspina in California,* fn. 51, p. 32.

There he reported Narváez' discoveries to Alejandro Malaspina,[2] who had arrived at the California capital five days earlier and did not leave for Acapulco until the 25th. Malaspina was impressed to learn that Narváez had probed deep into the northern arm of Juan de Fuca Strait, which seemed to continue a great distance. But Malaspina and his talented scientific officers reportedly were disappointed by the lack of detailed information provided by Carrasco. Apparently Narváez and Carrasco had not been meticulous enough about taking bearings or recording their explorations. Felipe Bauzá, who was in charge of charts and maps on Malaspina's voyage, believed that whenever Eliza turned in his finished charts, they wouldn't have much value for increasing geographical knowledge. José Bustamante, Malaspina's co-captain, apparently agreed.[3]

Throughout October and early November, Malaspina was in Acapulco and San Blas planning Spain's final quest for the elusive passage. On October 12, Malaspina wrote to the viceroy, informing him of Carrasco's report and proposing a follow-up expedition. After leaving Monterey October 16, Carrasco returned to San Blas November 9.[4] He delivered an extract of his voyage to Salvador Fidalgo, who forwarded it to the viceroy three days later. Carrasco also brought back fifteen Indian boys and seven girls who had been purchased with

---

[2]Malaspina, Alejandro, *Letter to Revilla Gigedo, San Blas,* October 12, 1791, in Correspondencia relativa a la expedicion de Malaspina, Tomo A, (583), Museo Naval, Madrid. See: Wagner, Henry R., *Spanish Explorations...*, p. 46; Cutter, Donald C., *Malaspina in California,* fn. 52, p. 32.

[3]Bauzá, Felipe, *Viaje alrededor del Mundo, 1789-96,* (749), MS in Museo Naval, Madrid; Bustamante, Jose, *Viaje de las Corbetas Descubierta y Atrevida a Montevideo, Chile, Peru, Acapulco y Filipinas—1789,* MS (13) in Archivo del Ministerio de Asuntos Exteriores, Madrid, as cited by Cutter, Donald C., *Malaspina in California,* fn. 54, p. 33. Note: Bauza, a top-flight geographer who eventually became director of the Deposito Hidrográfico in Madrid, may have exaggerated his apparent disdain for the pilots' talents. But it seems clear that Carrasco had not completed his chart at this time.

[4]Carrasco, op. cit., as translated by Wagner in op. cit., p. 202; Inglis, Robin, *Spain and the North Pacific Coast,* p. 186.

copper sheets. The expedition's officers and some of the men intended to educate and raise the youths. Carrasco returned 37 untraded copper sheets.[5]

At Nootka, Narváez, Verdía, and Pantoja labored over their charts, which were completed by October 15. Pantoja's *Pequeña costa que comprehende los interiores*... probably represents the original naming of places. Eliza delivered the charts to Bodega "well sealed and in good condition in some tin tubes."[6] On October 24, the *San Carlos* left Nootka carrying Eliza's report to the viceroy, which included charts drawn by Narváez and Pantoja. The vessel arrived in San Blas December 22. According to Pantoja, during the next seven days, he, Narváez, and Carrasco correlated "the plans and the descriptions" of Narváez' discoveries with those from the Quimper expedition. Presumably, this is when the comprehensive map was drawn, which is in Carrasco's distinctive handwriting. Pantoja was convinced the information would cause a revision in Malaspina's plans.[7]

After detailing the results of the expedition, Eliza made these comments about the Northwest Passage:

> If there is anything of particular importance or consideration to be explored on this coast it is this large canal. According to my method of thinking, and that of my pilot [Narváez], it promises much. . . . I assure your Excellency that the passage to the Atlantic Ocean, which foreign Nations search for with such diligence on this coast, cannot in my opinion, if there be one, be found in any other part; it is either, I think, by this great canal [i.e. behind the two 'islands' Narváez had sighted at the mouths of the Fraser River and Burrard Inlet], or it is a continent.[8]

When Viceroy Revilla Gigedo read this, his previously for-

---

[5]Wagner, Henry R., *Spanish Explorations*. . . , p. 34.

[6]Pantoja, Juan, *Extract of the navigation*. . . , as translated by Wagner in op. cit., p. 195.

[7]Pantoja, Juan, *Letter to Señor Don José de Prados y Salbatierra, written in San Blas,* Dec. 29, 1791, as translated by Wagner in op. cit., p. 199-200.

[8]Eliza, Francisco, *Extract of the voyage*. . . , as translated by Wagner in op. cit., p. 152.

mulated plan to complete the survey—spurred primarily by Malaspina—took on new urgency. For commander and pilot of the expedition, Malaspina initially had professed great confidence in the ability of three veteran mariners: Francisco Antonio Mourelle, Jacinto Caamaño, and Juan Carrasco. Mourelle and Caamaño were experienced San Blas officers who had sailed northward several times and were familiar with all the maps and accounts collected over the years. Carrasco had recently made the most complete chart of the Narváez expedition, incorporating information from the charts of Narváez, Pantoja, and López de Haro. The viceroy had actually placed Mourelle in charge of the expedition, which was ready to depart December 1.

But Malaspina soon changed his mind. Before leaving Mexico in early December on a voyage to the Marianas and the Philippines, Malaspina convinced Revilla Gigedo to send two of his recently promoted, most promising captains—Dionisio Alcalá Galiano and Cayetano Valdés y Bazan. Carrasco was replaced by the more versatile José Cardero. This draftsman turned "protoartist" was given the assignment of artist, scribe, journalist, map-maker, and pilot.[9]

On March 8, 1792, Captains Galiano and Valdés sailed from Acapulco aboard the schooners *Sutil* and *Mexicana* respectively. It marked the beginning of their famous voyage to the Pacific Northwest coast. They carried Carrasco's chart. The expedition led to their celebrated encounter with Captain George Vancouver on June 21st of that year near an anchorage in Georgia Strait recorded on Carrasco's map. In his journal, Galiano gave this account of the meeting:

> At seven in the morning a boat was sighted, which we did not doubt would be that of the English. It set course to come alongside, and

[9]Cutter, Donald C., *Malaspina and Galiano. . .* , p. 111-112; Cutter, Donald C., "*Jose Cardero: Protoartist. . .* ," p. 14; Inglis, Robin, *Spain and the North Pacific Coast,* pp. 186-189; Higueras, Maria Dolores, *Northwest Coast of America,* pp. 15-16.

Spanish stamps of 1967 honoring distinguished navigator Francisco Antonio Mourelle (1754–1825) (left), and Cayetano Valdés (1767–1839) (right). Mourelle was second pilot on second Bucareli expedition to explore the Pacific Northwest coast. The 1775 voyage was commanded by Bodega. In 1792, Valdés accompanied Dionisio Alcalá Galiano (1760–1805) on a voyage to the Pacific Northwest coast to resurvey Narváez' discoveries of 1791 using Carrasco's chart.

three officers came aboard this ship, being the commandant of the expedition, Mr. Vancouver, his lieutenant Mr. Puget, and a midshipman. They told us they had been engaged during the preceding days in exploring various inlets, and showed us [their] plans.... After seeing our map of the strait [Carrasco's], Mr. Vancouver reverted to the undertaking of joining the two expeditions.[10]

Vancouver wrote:

As we were rowing, on the morning of Friday the 22nd, we discovered two vessels at anchor under the land. These vessels, His Catholic Majesty's brig *Sutil,* under the command of Senor Don D. Galiano, with the schooner *Mexicana,* commanded by Senor Don C. Valdés, both captains of frigates of the Spanish navy, had sailed

[10]Kendrick, John (translator), *The Voyage of Sutil and Mexicana, 1792,* p. 131.

> from Acapulco on the 8th of March in order to prosecute discoveries on this coast. Sen. Galiano, who spoke little English,[11] informed me, that they had arrived at Nootka on the 11th of April, from whence they had sailed on the 5th of this month, in order to complete the examination of this inlet, which had, in the preceding year, been partly surveyed by some Spanish officers [Narváez et al] whose chart [Carrasco's] they produced.
>
> I cannot avoid acknowledging that, on this occasion I experienced no small degree of mortification in finding the external shores of the gulf had been visited [by Narváez] and already examined a few miles beyond where my researches during the excursion had extended.... Their conduct was replete with that politeness and friendship which characterizes the Spanish nation; every kind of useful information they cheerfully communicated, and obligingly expressed much desire, that circumstances might so concur as to admit our respective labours being carried on together.[12]

That event has taken precedence as the official date of "discovery" of the city now known as Vancouver. In fact, the *Santa Saturnina* was the first European vessel to sail upon the waters of English Bay and Burrard Inlet, making the 23-year-old Narváez and his crew the first white men to view the forest-clad north shore mountains that rose above what they thought might be the northern entrance to the Northwest Passage. In making his later surveys, Captain Vancouver would depend heavily on charts made on the Narváez expedition.

The author has translated and edited the original of Narváez' 1788 journal, located in the William Andrews Clark Memorial Library, which is connected to the University of California, Los Angeles. But the log of his 1791 voyage has never been found.[13] Narváez drew a chart of the Eliza expedition after it returned to Nootka. *Carta esferica que comprehende. . .*, with notations in Narváez' distinctively graceful

[11]Vancouver's chief Lieutenant, Peter Puget, said "this gentleman spoke English with great ease and fluency."

[12]Lamb, W. Kaye (editor), *The Voyage of George Vancouver 1791-1795*, p. 591-592.

[13]See Chapter 8.

Aboard Capt. Galiano's *Sutil* off Point Grey on June 21, 1792, a "mortified" Capt. Vancouver learns that Narváez had surveyed the area eleven months earlier. Oil by Ian Bateson, 1984. *Courtesy of City of Vancouver Archives.*

handwriting, shows the entire area investigated by the explorers. Dotted lines indicate the route that they travelled. A copy is in the Honnold Library in Claremont, California.

A far more detailed chart, drawn by Narváez' fellow pilot Juan Carrasco after he arrived in San Blas and possibly before he received Narváez' and Pantoja's charts, is located in Madrid's Museo Naval, Madrid. Titled *Carta que comprehende. . .*, it also shows Narváez' route. A note explains that tiny anchors indicate "good anchorages" and small "red squares at the edge of the coast are ranches of Indians." López de Haro, who had joined Carrasco in Spain's second exploration of Juan de Fuca Strait in 1790, also drew his chart in San Blas even though he did not go on the Eliza expedition. His *Plano reducido que comprende parte . . .* seems to have been copied from Pantoja's. Eliza filed a brief report of the expedition and the pilot Pantoja wrote extensively about the voyage. English translations of the reports and three charts (by Carrasco, Pantoja, and López de Haro) are contained in two books by Henry R. Wagner.[14] A large, clear reproduction of Carrasco's chart can be found in *Northwest Coast of America,* edited by Maria Dolores Higueras.

Carrasco was educated at the Academy of San Telmo in Spain for four and one-half years, sometime between 1775-80. He served in the Philippines under the highly skilled navigator Francisco Antonio Mourelle and came with him to the Pacific Northwest in 1784. After the Eliza expedition, Carrasco returned to San Blas, Mexico, in command of the *Santa Saturnina* and continued to serve from there as a pilot until at least 1803. The island in Juan de Fuca Strait now known as Protection Island was named Isla de Carrasco in 1790. Captain Vancouver renamed it two years later. The natives called it Chachanecuk. The Spanish also called Barkley Sound, on the west coast of Vancouver Island, Boca de Carrasco.

Today five inconspicuous locations remind British Columbians of Narváez' discoveries. In 1941, a cairn was erected in West Vancouver's Ambleside Park, incorrectly declaring that his expedition arrived there July 1, 1791. But the simple monument does indicate that it was Narváez, not Vancouver, who discovered the entrance to Burrard Inlet, which is now synonymous with Vancouver Harbour—one of the world's finest landlocked ports.

[14]*Cartography of the Northwest Coast of America* and *Spanish Explorations in the Strait of Juan de Fuca.*

A little plaque stands in the shadow of a stylized concrete anchor on Spanish Banks beach, marking Narváez' anchorage off Point Grey. The city of Vancouver memorializes its actual founder with only two place names: the one-block-long Narváez Drive, named in 1941, and Langara Golf Course, which took its name from the "islands" he charted. Finally, there is a single location in Georgia Strait commemorating its discoverer: tiny Narváez Bay at the south end of Saturna Island, the southernmost of the Gulf Islands, which was named after the *Santa Saturnina.*

After the Nootka Convention, Spain gave up her claim to America's northwest coast. In November 1791, Viceroy Revilla Gigedo had informed Malaspina that he intended to establish another outpost in Juan de Fuca Strait for fur trading when the one at Nootka was abandoned to the English.[15] But Spain failed to develop strong economic reasons for remaining at Nootka. Martínez had been the only Spanish mariner who recognized that fur trading would enable Spain to generate enough profits to offset the costs of maintaining a military presence. He had envisioned a monopoly company that would trade Mexican textiles and copper to the natives for naval supplies and furs, which would be sold in Canton for significant profits. Without such an economic base, Spain was incapable of taking on the task of converting the natives. Instead she sought negotiated frontiers that would protect her thinly settled missions in California. When Spain went to war against Britain and France in 1793, the Mexican viceroys had to devote more of their resources to defending the settled coasts of Mexico and California.

On July 20, 1792, Narváez was promoted to *piloto de segunda clase* (second pilot) and commissioned to make further mapping voyages along the Pacific Northwest coast using launches from the frigate *Concepción.* In April 1793, Narváez

[15]Inglis, op. cit., fn. 52, p. 197.

made his first voyage to Manila, carrying government documents aboard the frigate *San Jose de las Animas,* commanded by Caamaño.[16]

Spain signed a pact with England on January 11, 1794, renouncing her rights over Nootka. Britain sent out a representative to confirm the pact with a symbolic ceremony. Near the end of the year, Lieutenant Thomas Pearce of the Royal Marines arrived in San Blas, seeking passage to Nootka. He was transported there in January 1795 on the brigantine *Activo,*[17] commanded by Frigate Lieutenant Cosme Beltodano. Brigadier Colonel José Manuel de Alava, who had succeeded Bodega one year earlier, came aboard at Monterey, carrying the authority of the Spanish king. Narváez, appointed *piloto havilitado de primera clase* (qualified first pilot) the previous June 23rd, accompanied the expedition with orders to assist in the evacuation at Friendly Cove. He would remain a first pilot for the next twelve years.[18]

On March 28, 1795, Narváez saw the Spanish flag lowered and the English flag run up and down. Pearce gave the Union Jack to Maquinna, informing the chief that he was to hoist it whenever a ship sailed into Friendly Cove. Narváez supervised the destruction of the buildings he had helped erect, then he departed for San Blas aboard the *San Carlos* on April 16.

Spain's northernmost outpost on the Pacific coast had come to a quiet end. The natives set to work restoring their summer village site, salvaging bits of metal, planks, and anything else left behind by the Spaniards. They even dug up the cemetery and removed nails from coffins for conversion to fish hooks.[19]

---

[16]Marina de Guerra, *Estado de los méritos y servicios del Primer Piloto . . . Don José María Narváez,* p.3

[17]The 16-gun, two-masted, 200-ton brigantines were the eyes and ears of the Spanish empire. They were small, fast vessels that carried messages and official correspondence back and forth between Spain's far-flung establishments.

[18]Marina de Guerra, op. cit., p. 3.

[19]Archer, Christon I., "The Transient Presence," p. 31.

CALA DE LOS AMIGOS (FRIENDLY COVE), 1792
Engraving of a Harry Humphrys sketch, showing a three-masted British jolly boat under sail and the Spanish settlement on shore. Two hundred years ago this tiny cove was an international port frequented by sailing ships from many nations.
Courtesy of Vancouver Public Library, Photo #9565.

In December, Narváez made his second voyage to Manila to deliver government documents. He sailed aboard the *Activo,* commanded by Fidalgo. From Manila, he was ordered to carry other documents to warships in Macao. According to his service record, "he returned by the northeast past Hermosa Island [Taiwan] and the islands of Japan, a navigation entirely unknown to the Spaniards" up to that time.[20]

On October 23, 1796, at age 28, Narváez married María Leonarda Aleja Maldonado in the bride's hometown of

[20]Marina de Guerra, op. cit., p. 3.

Tepic, Mexico. Narváez' fellow pilot, José Verdía served as best man. For a time, the couple lived in San Blas before settling in Tepic. They would produce six boys and a girl. Narváez' great-great-great grandson—Jurist don José López Portillo—would serve as President of Mexico from 1976 to 1982.[21]

In 1797, Francisco Eliza, commander at San Blas, commissioned Narváez to make a topographic map of the entire territory that comprised the first militia division on the southern coast of New Spain. The chart was sent to Viceroy Marques de Branciforte.

Between February 1796 and December 1803, Narváez made military and diplomatic missions to Lima, Guayaquil, Panama, Loreto, and the four garrisons in Alta California. On June 17, 1804, he left San Blas for San Francisco, Monterey, Santa Barbara, and San Diego commanding the *Activo,* which was armed for war with 16 cannons. He carried orders to join the *Princesa* in halting "the contraband which strangers engage in on the coast."[22]

On October 20, 1806, Narváez became an *alférez de fragata* (frigate ensign). He would retain this rank for more than eleven years. Between 1805 and 1810, Narváez made several more supply voyages to the garrisons in Loreto and the Californias. Sometimes he commanded a ship, but he usually served as purser or captain's secretary.

In 1808, Narváez was commissioned to survey and construct a new road through the rugged mountains between San Blas and Tepic. After surveying the route that spring, Narváez started building the road during the summer. The grueling project forced him to endure blistering hot weather and a terrible infestation of insects. Road building continued through-

---

[21] See Appendix D for Narváez' genealogy.

[22] Marina de Guerra, op. cit., p. 3.

out the next year, but the undertaking would soon be interrupted by a popular rebellion that was spreading throughout Mexico.

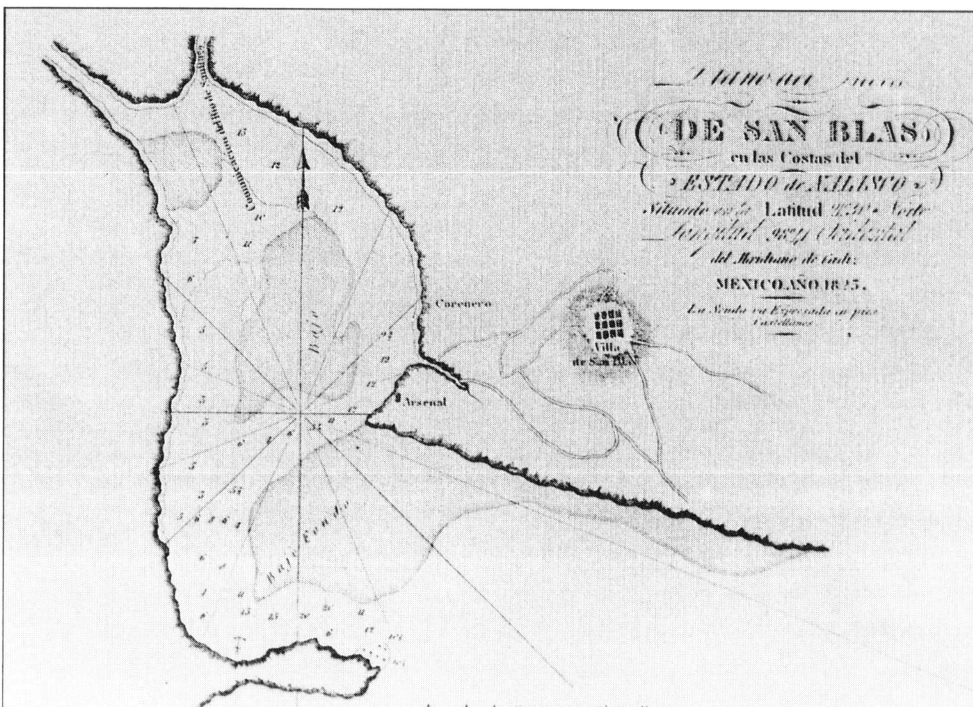

PLAN OF PORT SAN BLAS DRAWN BY JOSÉ MARÍA NARVÁEZ IN 1825.

CHAPTER 6

The Revolt of 1810 in New Spain

By 1800, a widespread desire for independence from Madrid had been building up momentum in New Spain for decades. The wellsprings of the rebellion were embedded in the caste system which the Spaniards brought with them to this part of their empire.

Throughout the seventeenth and eighteenth centuries, this rigid hierarchy had showed no signs of weakening. At the top were the *peninsulares*—those born in Spain. Their less fortunate countrymen called them *gachupines*, 'wearers of spurs.' They composed the smallest, richest, and most influential class. As a principle of colonial policy, Madrid tended to appoint these people to all important positions of responsibility. Most of the *gachupines* lived in Mexico City, Veracruz, and the major provincial towns.

The first conquistadors did not bring women with them, but Spanish women soon immigrated to New Spain. Within two or three generations, their offspring outnumbered the *gachupines* and resented them deeply because of their lock on power. These ambitious creoles formed the second most important class in terms of social and financial prestige. Their broad geographic distribution gave them widespread influence with the masses. Their erudite leaders were in contact with world-wide liberal ideological currents.

The third group were called mestizos. Born of Spanish and

Indian parents, they had almost no opportunity to rise socially or politically. But some became merchants and occasionally grew wealthy. Below them were eight or more castes, including mulattos—offspring of Spaniards and Blacks. At the bottom were zambos—the children of Blacks and Indians.

Creoles and mestizos would lead the struggle for independence from Spain, which had been smoldering for years. The creation of a caste system, Spanish exploitation of the Indians and the Blacks (who had been imported as slaves), and the restriction of employment to whites had sparked widespread discontent. The frustrated creoles had developed a strong sense of national identity and confidence in their collective future. They yearned for access to power, but they had limited sympathy for a violent uprising among the oppressed masses.

On September 16, 1810, a full-fledged revolt broke out when the maverick Catholic priest Miguel Hidalgo launched a poorly organized armed movement about 150 miles northeast of Mexico City. The white-haired priest was joined by a young military officer named Ignacio de Allende. Both men were liberal creoles. Support for the spontaneous uprising came largely from peasants and miners in the silver-rich Bajío region surrounding Mexico City. Many of these people were trying to escape virtual slavery. The growing horde of insurgents carried the banner of the brown Virgin of Guadalupe as their revolutionary symbol.

Hidalgo unleashed a highly charged rebellion against injustices. From the beginning, it took on the fervor and appearance of a religious crusade. The revolt spread rapidly and the untrained army expanded. When the rebel forces numbered 80,000, Hidalgo attacked Mexico City—the viceroy's seat of power. On the brink of capturing the city on November 3, Hidalgo inexplicably backed off. Temporarily, the movement lost its momentum.

But the desire to throw off the yoke of Spanish rule was not limited to the Bajío around Mexico City. Resentment ran high in Jalisco, especially in the capital city of Guadalajara. To lead the revolt in Jalisco, Hidalgo had managed to recruit José Antonio Torres, a mestizo administrator of a hacienda near Irapuato. On November 11, Torres met little resistance as he crushed ill-prepared royalist forces between Lake Chapala and Guadalajara, where Hidalgo was viewed as a liberator. Hidalgo must have been encouraged by Torres' easy victory and reports of the revolt spreading to other parts of the country. On November 26, Hidalgo entered Guadalajara at the head of a triumphal procession of some 7,000 followers.

Some of the revolt's strongest support came from creoles in the lower clergy. Because of their superior education and intimate contact with the Indians and Blacks, several priests of rural parishes became effective leaders of the peasant rebellion. In western Jalisco, one of them was Father José María Mercado, priest in Ahualulco, a small town about 50 miles due west of Guadalajara. After Torres took over that city, Mercado joined the cause and was responsible for spreading the uprising into Nayarit. On November 23, Mercado took Tepic and headed for San Blas. The poorly defended naval base, commanded by frigate captain José Joaquin Lavayen, offered the rebels an easy target.

Meanwhile, Narváez had returned to San Blas on November 1 in command of the *Activo*.[1] Everyone was talking about the popular uprising. *Gachupin* officials, merchants, veterans, and ranchers from Guadalajara westward to the Pacific coast feared for their lives and property. As the revolt spread, they gathered up whatever they could carry and fled to the military garrison at San Blas, where they sought refuge and an escape route by sea. The frightened elite would soon include two of

[1]Cárdenas de la Peña, Enrique, *San Blas de Nayarit,* Vol. 2, 117. Note: Much of the following narrative is based on this source, which in part summarizes the testimony given by Narváez and other officers at a subsequent military tribunal.

Guadalajara's most prominent citizens: Judge Juan Nepomuceno de Alva and Bishop Juan Cruz.[2]

On November 5, Commander Lavayen, who was in Tepic, ordered Narváez to arm the *Activo* for war and to load the ship with all the supplies it would carry in case a rapid retreat was required. On November 8, Lavayen arrived in San Blas and placed Lieutenant Jacabo Murphy, commander of the *San Carlos,* and Ensign Agustin Vocalán in charge of defending the establishment with the assistance of about 300 armed *gachupin* merchants, about 20 veterans, a number of ranchers on horseback, and about 200 unarmed sailors[3] from three ships: the frigate *Concepción,* the *Activo,* and the *San Carlos.* Narváez estimated that, in total, the defenders only had about 110 rifles and shotguns.[4]

According to Narváez, Lieut. Murphy was reluctant "to compromise himself by defending the town with people who lacked discipline and subordination." Narváez said three poorly armed, undermanned batteries were activated but not fully armed with cannons—San José on one side of Cristobal Bay, Castillo at the entrance, and Guadalupe near the Caracol arsenal.[5] Narváez warned Lavayen that even if artillery fire could be maintained, most of it would come from the two batteries flanking the bay, providing little defense from a land-based attack. He noted that the vulnerable Guadalupe battery, which had no cannons, could be taken by "any number of armed people."[6] Furthermore, the military had only been able to cut off one road with a trench.[7]

For about ten days the Spaniards sent out patrols to forage

[2]Ibid., 115.

[3]Ensign Felipe Garcia estimated 300 to 400 sailors. See: Cárdenas de la Peña, op. cit..., Vol. 2, 105.

[4]Cárdenas de la Peña, op. cit., Vol. 2, 117, 119. [5]Ibid., 117.

[6]According to Ensign Felipe Garcia, the town was sufficiently fortified with cannons in each of four or five batteries and on three ships in the bay. See: Cárdenas de la Peña, op. cit., Vol. 2, 105.

[7]Cárdenas de la Peña, op. cit., Vol. 2, 118, 119.

the surrounding area for food and supplies. But the men returned almost empty handed. The beleaguered Spaniards were running low on provisions. According to Narváez, about 70 water carriers and wood cutters had deserted the town. He said Spanish sailors weren't prepared to perform these essential tasks. When a squad of fully armed veterans was sent into San Blas on patrol, all the men fled to Tepic and joined the rebels. The *gachupin* volunteers constantly quarreled among themselves. Narváez was disgusted by their disorderly conduct and lack of discipline.[8]

One morning, the two companies of *gachupines* came close to waging a shootout because of a dispute over whether the Bishop of Guadalajara Juan Cruz, who had taken refuge aboard the *Activo,* should be brought ashore or not. They feared he would sail off and abandon them to the rebels.

"Their only interest was to save themselves and their possessions," said Narváez. He said one of the bishop's relatives, who was pastor of the cathedral of Guadalajara, had preached in San Blas about the need for the inhabitants to help defend the town from the rebels. But most of the townspeople had sided with Father Mercado.[9]

Lieut. Murphy, who had the thankless task of organizing the Spaniards into an effective defensive force, ended up screaming at them in frustration: "We were better defended when we were alone, than now that you have come."[10]

By November 25, the Spaniards realized they were surrounded by 2,000 to 6,000 rebels from 32 different towns. The insurgent force was within six miles of San Blas.[11] Narváez said the rebels were armed with spears, bows and arrows, rifles, and six cannons. To make matters worse, the armed company of turncoat veterans had decided to turn their guns against their countrymen.

[8]Ibid., 118.
[9]Ibid., 118, 119.
[10]Ibid., 118.
[11]Ibid., 105, 118-19.

On November 27, commander Lavayen shuffled his officers' responsibilities. He ordered Narváez to hand over command of the *Activo* to Lieut. Antonio Quartara and he replaced Murphy with Ensign Mateo Plowes as commander of Guadalupe battery.

On November 28, Father Mercado demanded that commander Lavayen surrender the Caracol fort and arsenal to the insurgents. As Lavayen's second in command, Ensign Vocalán negotiated the proposed terms with Mercado.

On November 30, commander Lavayen summoned Narváez, nine other naval officers, and leaders of the volunteers and veterans to two meetings. Lavayen told the men they had two choices. They could either surrender, or fight as long as possible and then retreat to the bay aboard the two brigantines and two merchant ships that were in port. The ships couldn't hold everyone, but many of them could escape with their lives. Lavayen read the four terms of surrender that Vocalán and Mercado had formulated and asked the officers to voice their opinions. Only three men—Plowes, Ensign Felipe Garcia, and a merchant named Carriaga—favored sinking the brigantines and defending the camp. Faced with this minority view, Lavayen asked the men to cast written votes. All but one of them voted for surrender.[12] Murphy abstained. Narváez said the Spanish position was hopeless.[13]

At about 11:00 P.M. that night, Narváez retired to his home in San Blas, convinced that Lavayen would not take any final action until the next day. But at 1:00 A.M. December 1, Ensign Garcia reported disturbing information to Narváez: Juan Echarte, captain of the civilian volunteers was preparing to escape by ship. Garcia suspected that all three vessels would

[12]Ensign Felipe Garcia said those who voted for capitulation based their decision on the apparent insubordination, lack of discipline, and unwillingness to wage a united defense among the civilian volunteers. See: Cárdenas de la Peña, op. cit., Vol. 2, 105.

[13]Cárdenas de la Peña, op. cit., Vol. 2, 105, 118-19.

slip away before dawn. To find out where things stood, the two men went to the commander's house, where they ran into Plowes and Vocalán. Lavayen said he had not ordered the ships to leave. By then it was 2:00 A.M., and Narváez reckoned it was too late for him to reach the ships. So he remained at the fort and waited for the inevitable surrender.[14]

Shortly after sunrise, Lavayen capitulated. According to Narváez, officers Plowes and Vocalán, along with civilian volunteers Francisco Pujadas (naval ministry administrator), José Monzón, and Marcelo Eroquer were all taken captive by the rebels to ensure that the surrender stuck. Because of their intercessions on behalf of the rebels, Vocalán and Andres Brillante, the customs house administrator in Guadalajara, apparently received preferential treatment.[15] San Blas—New Spain's most active west coast port—had fallen into rebel hands.

On January 17, 1811, Hidalgo's forces suffered a severe defeat near Guadalajara. The revolutionary army melted away. But the rebellion was not over. Scattered insurgent forces would maintain guerrilla warfare for the next decade.

Meanwhile, the royalist army was ready to regain control of other territory that had been lost to the rebels. On January 26, Brigadier José de la Cruz, Commander General of New Spain, left Guadalajara with a small force and set out to retake Tepic and San Blas. In Ahualulco, he issued a general pardon, then started hunting down rebels. At month's end, Mercado was gunned down in a ravine near San Blas. One week later Tepic was under royalist control. Insurgents came in droves to seek pardons. By mid-February, western New Spain from San Blas northward was pacified.[16]

---

[14]Ibid., 119.

[15] Ibid., 120.

[16]Alamán, Lucas, *Historia de México,* 1st ed, Vol. II, 141-49.

Narváez continued to serve the Spanish navy. But he was haunted by the spectre of being found guilty of treason for his part in the surrender of San Blas. In February 1811, commander Lavayen, Narváez, and nine other indicted officers were brought before a nine-judge military tribunal, which had been called by Brigadier Cruz.[17] Narváez and his colleagues stood accused of failing to defend the San Blas establishment vigorously enough during the early stages of the rebellion.

In his testimony, Narváez declared he had fulfilled his obligation to the viceroy by demonstrating no sympathy for the rebels and remaining in the service of the established government. "In my two assignments as commander of the brigantine *Activo* and as second in command of the battery commanded by Mateo Plowes, I always tried, in every way possible, to encourage naval personnel and other people to defend [the fort]," he said. The tribunal cleared all ten officers of any responsibility for the base being undermanned and poorly defended and for surrendering it to the rebels. Lavayen was ordered released from prison and he was restored to his post as commander at San Blas.

Following Hidalgo's disastrous defeat at Guadalajara, he and Allende went north toward what is now San Antonio, Texas, to reorganize the rebels. Pursued relentlessly by royalist soldiers, both rebel leaders were soon captured. Along with most of the revolutionists, Allende was shot in June. Turned over to the bishop of Durango, Hidalgo was defrocked, excommunicated, and then returned to Spanish authorities for execution. On July 30, 1811, he was shot by a firing squad. His revolutionary leadership had been brief. But he became known as the father of Mexican independence.

[17]Cárdenas de la Peña, op. cit., Vol. 2, 104 ff.

CHAPTER 7

Narváez Shifts His Allegiance

In 1813, Father José María Morelos continued the rebellion by organizing a successful uprising in southern Mexico. Unlike Hidalgo, he was a talented military tactician. Instead of heading up a large, unorganized army, which the Spaniards knew how to crush, Morelos methodically trained guerrilla bands to carry out hit-and-run attacks.

Morelos' vision for Mexico after independence was summed up in his constitution of 1814. It called for a democratically elected representative congress, a bureaucracy staffed by Mexicans, and equality under the law. It also abolished slavery, titles of nobility, government monopolies, sales taxes, and all forms of tribute. Morelos proposed a per capita income tax of five percent and an import duty of 10 percent. The *gachupines* and most creoles opposed these reforms, which were aimed at loosening their collective grip on political and economic power.

Narváez had set down roots in New Spain and, like many Spaniards, he had developed increasing interest in the general aims of creole reformers regarding independence. But he remained a royalist and continued to represent Spanish interests in the Pacific. From 1813 to 1814, he was put in charge of taking Spain's new, liberal constitution to Manila.

Meanwhile, the popular rebellion spread and Morelos gained control of most of southern New Spain. Brigadier Cruz was determined to smash the insurgency. Widespread support for the rebellion in the region convinced royalist commanders that the Indian population had to be repressed. To combat the rebels' guerrilla tactics, Cruz turned to draconian counterinsurgency measures and employed a wide range of coercive policies.

In 1815, Morelos was defeated, convicted of treason, and executed. Hidalgo had inspired the revolutionary movement; Morelos had given it purpose. Other guerrilla leaders carried on the struggle. Two of them were José Santana and creole Padre Marcos Castellanos. From 1813 to 1816, this pair spearheaded remarkably effective collective action by native people living around Lake Chapala at the head of the Santiago River.

This part of the popular struggle centered around the fortification and courageous defense of Mescala Island, a craggy, inhospitable volcanic island located about five miles into Lake Chapala near the hamlet of Tlachichilco. The rebels' decision to build a garrison there gave them a defensible base for launching effective guerrilla raids, provided a strategic advantage, and unified insurgent forces throughout the region. The insurgents' tenacious defense of the island fortress pitted untrained, poorly equipped Indian freedom fighters against the overwhelming firepower of disciplined, organized units of the royalist army which was backed by Spain's resources. The royalists' repeated failure to assault the base inspired the rebel cause during more than three years of bloody conflict.[1]

Helping Cruz crush this intense phase of the native rebellion was the last service Narváez would perform for the Spanish navy. In 1815, he was sent more than 200 miles inland to

[1]Archer, Christon I., "Rebellion in the Rebellion of New Spain," 18-19.

the royalist garrison at Tlachichilco,[2] where he joined five other experienced marine officers as launch skippers engaged in blockading Mescala Island and interdicting rebel raiders. Captain-Colonel José Navarro assigned each mariner two infantry officers. These officer teams and troops served eight-day rotations, with half the soldiers in patrol boats and the other half at Tlachichilco as a reserve division.[3] After taking other measures to strengthen the royalist forces, Cruz launched his final campaign of merciless, brutal repression.

Having seen royalist forces fail to storm Mescala Island at least four times at significant cost of men and equipment, Cruz was determined to starve out the island defenders by combining a tighter blockade with a ruthless scorched earth counterinsurgency policy around the entire lake. On November 25, 1816, Santana and Castellanos surrendered.

During the next year, whenever Narváez was not harassing Indian guerrillas and bandits or supplying Spanish outposts around Lake Chapala, he was expected to chart the lake and make a survey for a new road to Guadalajara. In recognition of his service during the Lake Chapala military campaign, Narváez received his stripes as *alférez de navio* (ship's ensign) on March 20, 1818. At the time, he was in the midst of mapping the entire province of Jalisco—a task which would take three more years.

By 1818, the royalists had pacified almost all of New Spain. But the viceroy's army was too fragmented, demoralized, and scattered among widely separated garrisons to quell another determined, sustained insurgency. Fortunately for the royalists, none occurred. The rebellion collapsed because the influential *gachupin* and creole elites failed to support it. Both saw their status, safety, and livelihoods were threatened if upris-

---

[2]Marina de Guerra, *Estado de los méritos y servicios del Primer Piloto...Don José María Narváez*, p.4

[3]Archer, Christon I., op. cit., p. 66.

ings of oppressed Indian and mestizo masses continued. But eight years of brutal war had already plundered the country, forged permanent enemies, and sowed seeds of chaos that would plague the country for generations.

Meanwhile, Narváez was still trying to remove any stain on his reputation left by the military trial that stemmed from the surrender of San Blas. In February 1820, Juan Villavicencio, Director General of the Armada in Cádiz, received a petition from Narváez, asking that he be given the Cross of the Royal and Military Order of San Hermenegildo for his performance during the fall of San Blas.[4] But the award was never granted.

The Spanish crown had been devoting most of its attention to defeating France and then trying to stabilize political control in the homeland after the war. With no direction coming from Madrid, factions in New Spain began to look for leadership at home. The man who emerged was Agustín de Iturbide, a young creole royalist captain who had helped defeat Morelos. This enthusiastic, spellbinding orator managed to convince rebel General Vicente Guerrero that winning independence was more important than achieving the aims of any single group. In February 1821, they agreed on a plan that guaranteed independence from Spain, equal rights for Spaniards and creoles, and supremacy of the Catholic religion. Then they formed a common army. Seven months later, Iturbide marched into Mexico City, proclaimed Mexico's independence, and started to set up what would turn out to be a brutal, but short-lived empire.

With the end of Spanish rule, Narváez decided to remain in Guadalajara with his family. Madrid accepted his "retirement without gain of salary," but the Spanish Navy would not discharge him officially until May 25, 1825.[5] Meanwhile, Narváez was named speaker of Guadalajara's auxiliary consul-

---

[4]Marina de Guerra, op. cit., p. 16-17.

[5]Ibid., p. 20-22.

tative junta and later elected by popular vote as Provincial Deputy to Iturbide's provisional government.

One of the first steps taken by Iturbide was organization of a Mexican Navy. In December 1821, on Iturbide's recommendation, Narváez was appointed *teniente de fragata* (frigate lieutenant)—a rank achieved in the Spanish Navy by very few former pilots.

In May 1822, Iturbide ordered Narváez to take command of the brigantine *San Carlos* in San Blas and sail to Baja and Alta California with Canon Don Agustín Fernandez of San Vicente, who had been commissioned to set up a new administration there. Narváez helped to install commissions and councils in both provinces. This was the first of several important assignments that Narváez would carry out for successive Mexican governments.

Meanwhile, Iturbide stunned even his most ardent supporters by declaring himself Emperor Agustín of Mexico. But eight months later, he was overthrown by a liberal revolt and exiled. Iturbide's successor was the even more devious General Antonio López de Santa Anna. Mexico would adopt a constitutional government, but General Santa Anna found extralegal ways to influence governmental decisions.

On March 9, 1823, following his return from the Californias, Narváez was made Commandant of the Department of San Blas—still the most important port on Mexico's western coast. Although he was sent off on other temporary assignments, he would remain in this position until October 30, 1827, when the post was suspended due to funding cuts.

In December 1824, Guadalupe Victoria, a distinguished jurist, became Mexico's first president. Narváez was ordered to take command of the bilander *Mexicana* so he could reconnoiter and map the coast between the ports of San Blas and Manzanillo. When Narváez finished this task, José Joaquin de Herrera, General Commandant of Jalisco, sent him to

Colima so he could correct the locations of some towns between that city and Guadalajara on the map of Jalisco, which he had completed three years earlier.

By April 1825, Narváez had worked his way up to *capitán de fragata* (a junior captain). He returned to his post at San Blas. That same year, Narváez supplied the government with maps he had drawn of the border areas with Louisiana and Texas. He also supervised construction of schooners for Mexico's mail service to the Californias. In 1826, Narváez became a founding member of an Institute of Science, Literature and the Arts.

At the end of October 1827, Narváez lost his command but continued living in Tepic as a civilian. But on November 3, he wrote to President Guadalupe Victoria, saying he could not support his family on the skimpy navy pension he had been allotted. He was granted permission to work at half pay on coastal merchant ships. But two years later, he was writing the President again, this time for back pay he was owed from his last year as commandant at San Blas. He had insisted that all the local day laborers be paid first, and the government ran out of money before it could pay Narváez.

In 1830, Narváez drew a map of Alta California,[6] which showed the coastal area between "Estableamiento Ruso" (Fort Ross) in the north and Mission San Miguel in the south divided into four districts: San Francisco, Monterey, Santa Barbara, and San Diego. According to Narváez, about 20,000 native "converts" inhabited 19 missions and approximately 4,500 troops and unconverted people were scattered around presidios, towns, and ranches. He estimated the total population at 23,676. East of the coastal range of mountains, Narváez' map showed the vast "Cienegas ô Tulares"—seasonal wetlands that in years of heavy rain filled the Mexican

[6]Narváez, José María, *Plano del territorio de la Alta California . . . 1830,* #392 M, Bancroft Library, University of California, Berkeley; Thelander, Carl G., *Life on the Edge,* p. 170.

province's large central valley with a great, shallow inland sea which covered more than 700 square miles. At that time, it was the largest body of fresh water west of the Great Lakes.

Following 49 years of naval service, Narváez retired completely April 20, 1831, at the age of 63 and settled in Guadalajara. He was granted a meager pension of 141 pesos, six reales and eight granos.

In early 1840, Narváez produced a scaled down version of the map of Jalisco that he had completed earlier. It included what are now the states of Jalisco, Nayarit, Colima, Zacatecas, and Aguascalientes. Antonio Escobedo, Governor of Jalisco, sent the map to Europe for engraving. Two years later, it became Jalisco's first official map. In 1852, it was published in New York, but Narváez was already dead.

The distinguished mariner who had adopted Mexico as his homeland died Aug. 4, 1840 in Guadalajara at age 72. His family possessed several original maps, charts and notes, including, probably, his log of the Gran Canal voyage.

One authority claims to have seen the log during the last year of Narváez' life. In 1839, Eugene Duflot de Mofras, a member of the French embassy in Madrid, was given the assignment of surveying New Spain and the Pacific Northwest for France. In the English translation of his book *Travels on the Pacific Coast,* he mentions that "in 1840 Don José Narváez brought out his Journal and the original charts of his interesting voyage for our inspection."[7] Duflot de Mofras seems to have been referring to the Mexican mariner's exploration of Juan de Fuca Strait in 1789, but Narváez discussed several voyages with him, including the one in 1791.[8] The reference to more than one chart is also noteworthy. Most important, this confirms that Narváez, unlike most officers, kept these important documents and possibly many others.

---

[7]Duflot de Mofras, Eugene, *Travels on the Pacific Coast,* fn. 64, p. 63.

[8]Ibid., p. 63-64 and Duflot de Mofras, Eugene, *Exploration du territoire de L'Oregon, des Californies, et de la Mer Vermeille,* vol. 2, p. 131.

Narváez' family offered to give the noted hydrographer's historic documents to the Mexican government in exchange for about six thousand pesos in back pay. But their offer fell on deaf ears. Narváez died forgotten and poor.[9] History had passed him by.

[9]Otero, Mariano, *Obras del Sr. Licenciado Mariano Otero,* Vol. 1, pp. 62-63.

CHAPTER 8

Narváez' Missing Journal of 1790-1791

In the past century, historians have searched in vain for the journal that Narváez wrote on his important voyage of discovery in 1791 at age 23. Although it is not needed to confirm the young navigator's remarkable achievements, it would probably clarify significant details of the expedition. It is also a key document for gaining a full understanding of that pivotal period in Pacific Northwest Coast maritime history when political and military control shifted from Spain to England and the United States.

Following the leads of previous investigators, the author has made the most intensive search to date for this document. It is not catalogued in any library in Mexico, Spain, the United States, or Canada. It seems to have been in Narváez' possession at the time of his death in 1840.[1] The Mexican government apparently did not purchase Narváez' journals, charts, and other papers at that time. Because his family was eager to sell these documents, it is highly probable that they were purchased by a private collector. If that happened, such a collector probably purchased both the log Narváez wrote in 1788 and the one he recorded in 1791.

To investigate that possiblity, the author traced the route by

[1]See the last two paragraphs of chapter seven.

which Narváez' log of 1788 was obtained by the William Andrews Clark Memorial Library. This archive was founded by William Andrews Clark, Jr., and bequeathed in 1934 to the University of California at Los Angeles as a memorial to his father, W. A. Clark (1839-1923)—the wealthy, influential Montana copper-mining magnate and U.S. Senator.

The author found an interesting letter in W.A. Clark, Jr.'s, correspondence files dated December 1, 1933, from Henry R. Wagner—the American historian who did most of the seminal research about Spanish exploration of the Pacific Northwest coast. The letter indicates that Clark purchased the 1788 manuscript and several other Mexican documents as a small block from Dr. Abraham S.W. Rosenbach "a few years ago" (i.e. the early 1930s). During the first half of the 20th century, Rosenbach was the leading North American book and document seller.

David Szewczyk—now owner of The Philadelphia Rare Books and Manuscripts Company in Philadelphia, Pennsylvania—once worked as a curator for the Rosenbach Foundation and was in charge of Rosenbach's Mexican collection. In 1980, Szewczyk wrote *The Viceroyalty of New Spain and Early Independent Mexico: A Guide to Original Manuscripts in the Collections of The Rosenbach Museum and Library.*

According to Szewczyk, Rosenbach probably obtained the small block of Mexican manuscripts that he sold to Clark from a Philadelphia lawyer by the name of George H. Hart, whose collection was sold in 1922. Lot 801 in that sale was titled: *Mexico: An extensive collection of official manuscript documents relating to Mexico, the Inquisition, legal cases, etc. from the late 18th century up to the period of the Mexican War.*

Szewczyk believes that Hart probably obtained this large block of Mexican manuscripts at a Bangs & Company auction held June 19-23, 1893, in New York City, during which 3,005 lots of Mexican materials collected by Henry Ward Poole were sold. Lots 1-2939 contained books and manuscripts.

"Poole was one of the least known but most colorful and important 19th century collectors of Mexicana," wrote Szewczyk. In 1856, he landed in Veracruz as a surveying engineer for the Mexican Pacific Coal and Iron Mining and Land Company. In 1857, he returned to the United States. The following year, he went back to Mexico to teach at the College of Mines. He worked there until his death in 1890. When not teaching, Poole collected books, manuscripts, and historical paintings.

In 1869 or 1870, Poole decided to sell his library. He shipped it to Boston, where it was sold in 1871. The sale catalogue listed 973 lots.

From 1874 to 1882, Poole built another enormous Mexican collection containing about 10,000 *legajos* (dossiers). "The bulk of the Rosenbach Mexican manuscripts comes from this second collection," wrote Szewczyk in 1980.[2]

After Poole died, his brother, William Frederick Poole, arranged for the sale of Poole's second collection at the 1893 auction mentioned above. W.F. Poole was librarian of the Boston Athenaeum and the Newberry Library and president of the American Hisorical Association and of the American Library Association.

As an annotated copy of the sale catalogue for the Bangs & Co. auction has not been located, the identities of the buyers remain a mystery. Szewczyk believes W.F. Poole probably acquired some items for the Newberry Library or for collector Edward E. Ayer. *A CheckList of Manuscripts in the Edward E. Ayer Collection,* by Ruth Lapham Butler, does not list either of Narváez' logs.

Szewczyk also believes that dealers such as Lathrop Harp-

[2]Szewczyk, David, *The Viceroyalty...*, xi.

er purchased most of the manuscript lots at the Bangs & Co. auction. The author was unable to find either of Narváez' logs listed in Lathrop Harper catalogues after 1920.

"Most of the Poole manuscripts disappeared," wrote Szewczyk. A portion re-emerged in the library of George H. Hart."[3]

According to Szewczyk, Rosenbach may have removed and sold separately certain documents that he acquired in the Hart auction. We now know that it was exactly in this manner that Clark obtained Narváez' log of 1788. But in December 1993, responding to an inquiry from the author, Szewczyk said he could not find any record of the purchase of the 1788 log by Clark from Rosenbach nor "any evidence that the 1791 manuscript was part of Poole's collection."

In January 1994, at the author's request, Elizabeth Fuller, curator at the Rosenbach Foundation, made an extensive search of the foundation's catalogs and of Rosenbach's correspondence. She reported finding isolated references to different lots of Mexican documents but no itemization of either of the Narváez manuscripts.

So, the author reached another dead end in the quest for the original of the missing log. If the document exists in North America, it may be buried among the acquisitions of some private collector who obtained it in the early 1900s. Or it could be lost forever.

But this does not mean that the search must end. If the original manuscript cannot be located, there is still the possibility of finding a copy. During the exploration period, the Spanish navy was strict about requiring all captains and pilots of expeditions to file their original journals or copies thereof with the Viceroy in New Spain and with Madrid. This means that an official copy should still reside in one of the Mexican or Spanish archives.

[3] Ibid., xii.

Other researchers have probed the catalogued materials in these archives for the manuscript in question without success. But the large number of uncatalogued materials that are located in the Archivo General and the Biblioteca Nacional in Mexico City require further investigation.

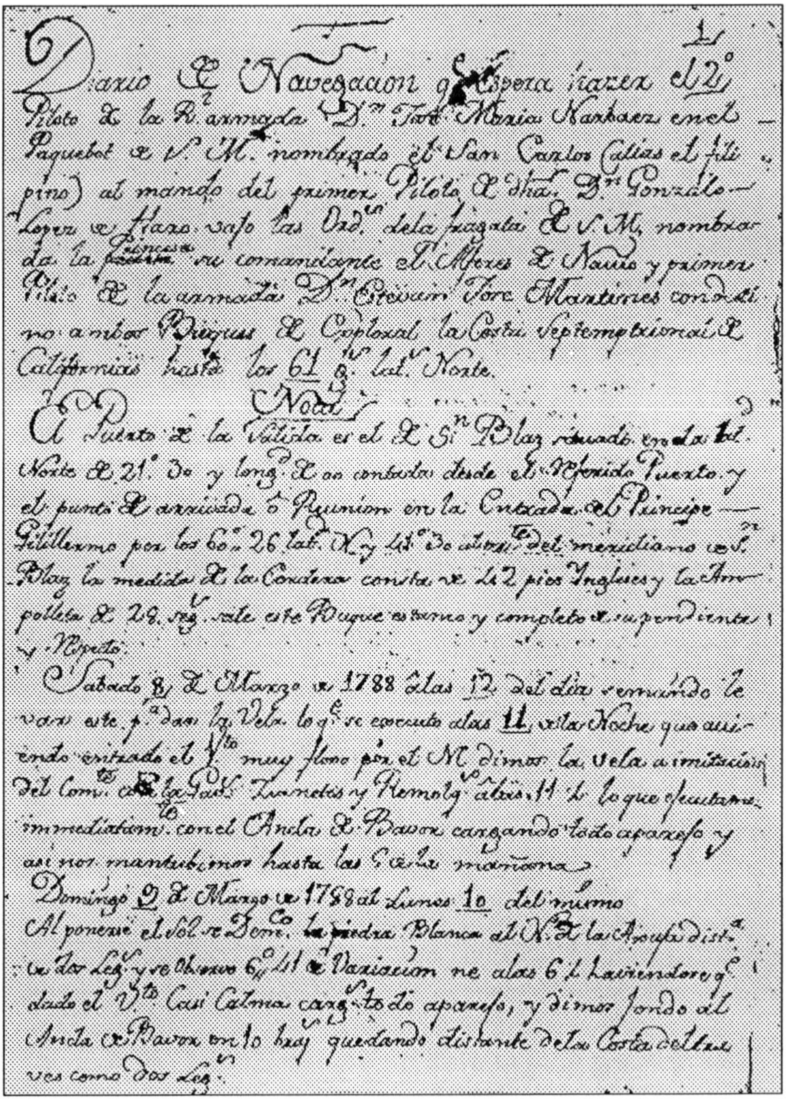

Diario de Navegacion que espera hazer el 2º Piloto de la R.l armada D.n Josef Maria Narbaez en el Paquebot de S. M. nombrado el San Carlos (alias el Filipino) al mando del primer Piloto de dha. D.n Gonzalo Lopez de Haro, bajo las Ord.es de la fragata de S. M. nombrada la Princesa su comandante el Alferez de Navio y primer Piloto de la armada D.n Estevan Jose Martinez con destino ambos Buques de explorar la Costa Septemptrional de Californias hasta los 61 g.s lat. Norte.

FIRST PAGE OF NARVÁEZ JOURNAL OF 1788.

CHAPTER 9

Narrative of the Voyage, 1788

In 1774, '75 and '79, Spain sent expeditions from San Blas northward to investigate Alaskan waters, look for Russian fur traders, and search for the Northwest Passage.[1] *But the Spanish mariners found neither Russians nor the legendary shortcut to Europe. For the next nine years, Spain was forced to concentrate most of her resources and naval talent on war with England. Exploration of America's northwest coast seemed much less urgent. But when the French explorer Jean-Francois Lapérouse arrived in Concepción de Chile in February 1786 after a brief exploratory voyage to the Pacific Northwest coast, he sparked new interest in Alaska among the Spaniards. Lapérouse carried a general map showing four Russian establishments in Alaska, one of which was at Nootka. Madrid ordered an immediate investigation.*

As we have seen, this led to Narváez' first assignment on an expedition to the Pacific Northwest coast. What follows is the first complete English translation of the journal that he kept on that voyage. Working from the original journal,[2] *the author and his wife produced the following annotated narrative.*[3]

---

[1]Thought to have been somewhere in latitude 60° on the northwest coast of America.

[2] Located at William Andrews Clark Memorial Library, Los Angeles, California.

[3]For translating Spanish words, the primary reference was *Cassell's Spanish Dictionary*. Unless otherwise noted, the names of people in the manuscript are those used by Narváez. Place names capitalized in the manuscript have been translated. Present day equivalents for the places named are given either in brackets [ ] or in footnotes. To avoid ambiguity or clarify the apparent meaning, some English words have been inserted by the translator and enclosed in brackets [ ]. The same is done with a few dates. To convert the mariner's log into readable

Log of navigation[4] that Don José María Narváez, Second Pilot of the Royal Armada, intends to make in the packet-boat of His Majesty, named *San Carlos* (alias *Filipino*) commanded by Don Gonzalo López de Haro, First Pilot of the Armada, under the orders of the frigate of His Majesty named *Princesa*, commanded by Don Estevan José Martínez, Ensign of the Navy and First Pilot of the Armada,[5] with the destination of both ships to explore the northern coast of the Californias to 61°[6] of latitude north.[7]

Note: The port of departure is San Blas, situated at 21°30'N of latitude and 00°00" of longitude, counted from that port to the point of [anticipated] arrival or reunion at the entrance of Prince William Sound at 60°26' N of latitude and 41°30' of longitude west[8] of the San Blas meridian. The measure of the

---

prose, minor changes of syntax have been made throughout the manuscript. The surprisingly few errors made by Narváez and a few unreadable notes in the margin have been ignored.

4*Diario el Navegacion que Espera Haser el 2nd Piloto de la Real Armada Don José María Narbaez en el Paquebot el* S.M. Nombrado el San Carlos *comandado por el 1st Piloto López de Haro* . . . , 1788. Diary of Navigation that Don José María Narváez, Second Pilot of the Royal Armada expects to make in the Packetboat *San Carlos,* commanded by López de Haro, First Pilot. . . , 1788 (MS Mex N238M3 D539 [1788]), William Andrews Clark Memorial Library, Los Angeles, California.

5The orders, issued January 25, 1787 in Madrid and again July 24, directed José Camacho, senior first pilot and commandant at San Blas, to dispatch two ships with his best pilots. But Camacho had no first rank officers on hand. The initial orders designated Camacho and Francisco Mourelle to lead the expedition, originally scheduled to leave in January 1788. But Mourelle was in Manila. On November 28, 1787, Camacho informed the Viceroy that he was too sick to go. On December 18, the Viceroy made two new appointments: Martínez took Camacho's place and López de Haro replaced Mourelle, who had not returned.

6The expedition of 1779 had returned convinced that a high range of mountains (the present Chugach Mountains) rose behind Prince William Sound, barring the possibility of reaching 70°N, as it had been instructed.

7Commander Martínez was accompanied by pilot Antonio Palacios, second pilots Antonio Serantes and Estevan Mondofía, surgeon Diego Muñoz, chaplains José López de Nava and José María Diaz, and an 89-man crew. Serving under second-in-command López de Haro were two pilots—Narváez and Juan Martínez y Zayas, *pilotin* José Verdía, chaplain Nicolas Loera, and a crew of 83. Almost all of the sailors were Mexican: mestizos, Indians, mulattos and blacks.

8When referring to longitude from San Blas, Narváez starts out using *or*. . . and then uses *o*. . . in the rest of the manuscript. Either of these could be shorthand for *oriente* (east) or *oeste*

log-line consists of 42 English feet and the hour glass of 28 seconds.[9] Therefore, this ship is seaworthy and its inspection is complete in all respects.

SATURDAY, MARCH 8, 1788. At 12:00 noon, [I] was ordered to set sail in this ship [and] to observe what was seen.[10] At 11:00 that night, having a fresh wind from the north, we kept watch along with the Lieutenant Commander [of the expedition]. At 11:00 P.M., we dropped the port anchor and stayed there until 9:00 A.M.

SUNDAY, MARCH 9 TO MONDAY, MARCH 10. At sunset, the White Rock[11] appeared about two leagues[12] away. [The

(west). With respect to longitude, the expedition was clearly *west* of San Blas throughout the voyage. So the translator has used west in all references to longitudinal distances from San Blas. For the sake of consistency, the translator has also interpreted *o...* to mean west wherever it appeared, as long as the context supported this interpretation. Brackets [] indicate where this was done.

[9]Knots were spaced 42 feet or seven fathoms apart on the log-line. Assuming there was no slip when the log was streamed, the line would spool out at the rate of 42 feet per each 28 seconds measured by the hour glass. In one hour, this would give a length of about 5,400 feet—approximately 10 percent less than the true value of 6,076 feet in a nautical mile. There was always some slip, because the log board had to be pulled through the water to spool out the line. French mariners estimated five percent. It is unclear why the Spanish used 10 percent.

[10]During the first period of discovery on the Northwest Coast (prior to the Malaspina expedition of 1791-92), the cartographic work of drawing up charts was generally left to the ship's pilot. Most of these men were from the pilot's school of San Telmo and lacked scientific training in nautical astronomy, which was not needed because maps were not yet drawn using astronomical methods. Frequently these pilots did not sign their charts, but the maps provided the cartographic foundation for all of Spain's intensive exploration in the region.

Senior officers were responsible for recording astronomical observations to pinpoint places on the coasts. Lacking precision instruments, they relied heavily on dead reckoning. Recorded latitudes were often arrived at by averaging the observations of pilots and officers.

By 1788, for basic hydrographic work, a vessel was supposed to carry: two azimuth compasses to take exact bearings, observe variation and take bearings on land; three sextants to observe latitude and longitude; a graduated semicircle with a radius of one foot and a plane table for surveying short coastlines. To make the exact observations of latitude and longitude of main points needed to chart longer coastlines, the following astronomical instruments were required: an astronomic pendulum, a quadrant with a two-and-a-half-foot radius and two telescopes with a 24-inch focus. (See: Martín-Merás, Luisa, "The Evolution of Spanish Cartography on the Northwest Coast of America," in *Spain and the North Pacific Coast*, edited by Robin Inglis, p. 19.)

[11]A landmark by which the port of San Blas was recognized.

[12]Six nautical miles.

sun] was observed at 06°41' of variation NE. At 6:00, the wind having become almost completely calm, we lowered the port anchor about two leagues from the coast.

MONDAY, MARCH 10. At 6:00 A.M., we sighted the Marías Islands.[13] At sunrise, the middle isle[14] appeared to the [west] and the southernmost one was S 80° [W], about six leagues from the former.

TUESDAY, MARCH 11. At sunrise, we sighted the Islas Marías to the north at a distance of five or six leagues.

WEDNESDAY, MARCH 12. At noon, we arrived at the Islas Marías and continued [on our way]. At sunset, [the sun] was observed at 05°08' of variation NE.

MONDAY, MARCH 17. At sunrise, [the sun] was observed at 05°05' of variation NE.

SUNDAY, MARCH 30. At sunrise, [the sun] appeared at 06°11' of variation NE.

THURSDAY, APRIL 10. At sunrise, [the sun] was observed at 08°30' of variation NE.

FRIDAY, APRIL 11. At sunrise, [the sun] was observed at 08°05' of variation NE.

WEDNESDAY, APRIL 16. At 9:00 A.M., the commander put his launch in the water and, as we were nearby, the frigate's launch headed for our ship with an officer. He brought instructions about the points to which we were supposed to direct ourselves in case of separation [before] arrival at some port, [and about] the precautions we should observe in case of meeting foreign ships at sea. At the same time he instructed us to follow the route toward the northwest running to the landfall on the coast. At 10:00, the officer returned to his ship. At 10:15, [both ships] left under full sail without further delay.

MONDAY, APRIL 21. At sunrise, [the sun] was observed at 11°00' variation NE.

---

[13]A group of four islands that include the *Tres Marías:* (N to S) San Juanito Island, María Madre Island, María Magdalena Island, María Cleofas Island.

[14]María Magdalena Island.

FRIDAY, APRIL 25. At 5:30, we remained becalmed. During the afternoon, various black birds passed by, suggesting [an ominous destiny] and bad waters.

SATURDAY, APRIL 26. At 2:00, various ducks swam by and many other black birds. The wind diminished toward the SW ¼ W.

SUNDAY, APRIL 27. At 5:00, five wolf-fish[15] passed, staying near the ship's side for a long while.

Note: For the last 24 hours the water has had a blue-green color. Various ducks have passed sitting on the water and wolf-fish. Yesterday, a sounding was taken at 6:00 P.M.

MONDAY, APRIL 28. In the afternoon, we saw different types of flying birds.

TUESDAY, APRIL 29. At 11:00 A.M., a band of ducks passed by.

SATURDAY, MAY 3. At 4:00, a dense fog rolled in. At 6:00, the commander fired a loud cannon shot to indicate his location. Hour by hour, we followed his signals.

MONDAY, MAY 5. At 10:00, during a forceful gale of wind, the bottom of the mizzen mast broke in two under the boom joint. So we immediately took charge and continued with the extra job of demasting her and putting the mast below.

WEDNESDAY, MAY 7. The boom was ready and the mizzen mast was fastened to the mainmast.

THURSDAY, May 8. During the afternoon, an endless number of sea gulls and some black birds and whales passed by.

FRIDAY, MAY 9. At 3:00 P.M., the anchor remained fastened to the cable.[16]

SATURDAY, MAY 10. At sunset, [the sun] was observed at 21° of variation NE.

[15]Seals, sea otters, or sea lions.

[16]111¼ fathoms long.

SUNDAY, MAY 11. This afternoon, we saw various sticks float by.

WEDNESDAY, MAY 14. By sunset, nothing new had happened. During the afternoon, we saw an endless number of birds. Among them were little ducks with very red beaks.[17] I noticed one or two flying ones in the water, like those one finds on beaches or sand banks. In the morning, there was a heavy mist. At sunrise, there was nothing new in the variation. The color [of the sea] continued to be mixed. Sea birds and many whales were active.

THURSDAY, MAY 15. We made repairs. The water being blue-green, we threw in the leadline but found no bottom. At 6:00 P.M. numerous sticks passed by. One of them had a rope attached. At 8:15, the commander, being nearby, signaled us to lay to our foresail and mizzenmast. We estimated we were about nine leagues from Lower Pamplona, which was discovered by the Spaniards in 1779.[18] At 7:00 A.M., we saw land off the starboard bow. It was obscured by the heavy fog that hung over it. We signaled to the commander.

FRIDAY, MAY 16. At midday, we continued along the coast under fullest possible sail, following the route to the N ¼ NW and NNW for 3½ leagues. Arriving at the coast, the commander signaled to us to tack by resounding, which we did. At the same time we anchored in 68 fathoms, with a mud bottom. The commander called to ask us the latitude we had observed at midday and that at which we had arrived. We responded that the latitude observed was 59°46' N, that the land seemed to us to be Montague Island, and that the open-

---

[17]Possibly mergansers.

[18]Although Narváez followed Cook's map and used many of his names, he clearly had a Spanish map from the 1779 expedition led by Ignacio de Arteaga and Juan Francisco de la Bodega. It was probably the *Carta Reducida*. . . , drawn by Arteaga's first pilot José Camacho, commandant at San Blas in 1788. On either July 15 or 17 of that year, the Arteaga-Bodega expedition sighted a reef 12 leagues from the coast at 59°02' of latitude and 40°34' of longitude, which they named *Pamplona*.

ing to the north was the entrance of Prince William Sound.[19] The commander responded that we should continue sounding under sail and reconnoiter the island that we had seen. At sunset, the point [of land] to the north was to the W ¼ SW about five or six leagues away.

Until dark, we did nothing else except sound from time to time in six fathoms. At 4:00 A.M., the rest of Montague Island appeared to the W ½ NW about four to 4½ leagues away. We arrived there at noon.

Note: Yesterday, at 3:00 P.M., we agreed that the lands we had glimpsed were Montague Island and the continental coast at the entrance into Prince William Sound. After charting the southernmost point south of Montague Island to the west at a direct running distance of five leagues, we found that this island was actually 40 leagues farther west of the ship than the bearing shown on the Spanish chart of 1779.[20]

In resolving my longitude with that of the Greenwich meridian used on Cook's chart, I estimated that he found his ship situated eight nautical miles more to the west [when he located Montague Island]. From this day forward, I will continue working from this [location], converting his longitude to that of the San Blas meridian in order to see if this chart is more accurate than the Spanish one.

SATURDAY, MAY 17. At noon, we were at 59°47'N of latitude and bearing on Montague Island at an angle of 29°04' on the quintant.[21] I believe the true longitude was 41°30' west of San Blas. At sunset, I saw the point that was north of the [eastern] entrance[22] to Prince William Sound along with Montague Island. The entrance was to the N 47° W and the

---

[19]The present Hinchinbrook Entrance.

[20]The dispute about which island they had found would open a serious rift between most of the pilots and Martínez. See fn. for entry of June 1.

[21]A navigational and astronomical instrument divided into 72° instead of the 60° of the sextant, so it could measure an angle of 144°.

[22]Hinchinbrook Strait.

point north of Montague Island was to the N 61° W. The farthest north one could see into Prince William Sound was to the N 64° W about three or four leagues from [Montague Island]. At sunrise, I saw the point that was north of the entrance to Prince William Sound and north of Montague Island to the NW ¼ W about four or five leagues away from [Montague Island]. At 7:15 A.M., it was completely calm.

SUNDAY, MAY 18. At noon, according to my observation, we were at 59°92'N of latitude and Montague Island was farther north at an angle of 15°04'. I estimated the true longitude was 41°38' west of San Blas.

At midday, we continued with only sea gulls between us and the entrance of Prince William Sound. There was absolutely no wind. At 12:00 [noon], the commander called out that we should immediately reverse our course because we were completely becalmed. At 3:00, his boatswain arrived in the ship's boat with a message for the captain. At 9:00 [P.M.], the boat left with the captain's answer. At sunset, the point north of Prince William Sound was to the N 31° and the northernmost part of Montague Island was to the south 74° W, about four leagues away. At this hour, we were in 68 fathoms, with a bottom of loose mud.

At sunrise [May 19], the point north of Prince William Sound was to the N 29° W and the south point of Montague Island was to the WSW 09° W about four leagues away. At 6:00, there was an opening to the west-northwest so we tacked to the outside.

MONDAY, MAY 19. At noon, I observed we were at 59°40'N of latitude. At the same time, the southeasternmost part of Montague Island was to the W 08' running. By this information, I believed the true longitude was 42°28' west of San Blas. At sunset, the point north of Prince William Sound was to the N 30° W and the southernmost point of Montague Island was to the South 65° W, about four or five leagues from the coast. At 10:00 P.M., the weather was good, the horizon overcast and it was calm. The commander was off the starboard bow a short distance. Until dawn, the winds blew lazily in gusts from the northwest to the NNE, so we tacked south with the aim of separating ourselves from the island. At dawn, the sky was clear, the horizon was misty, the wind was lazy and [the sea was] flat. At 3:00 A.M. [May 20], the commander signaled us to head S 76° toward Montague Island, which was about five leagues away. Shortly thereafter, we discovered the little Navzas Islands. The twins ran northwest to southeast. They are situated about 10 leagues southeast of Montague Island. According to my estimate, they are at 59°30' N of latitude. The commander named them Hijosa Islands.[23] Together they are about four or five leagues long. These islands are not marked on Cook's chart nor on the Spanish one [of 1779]. At 10:00, with the wind blowing toward the northeast, we raised our mainsails and starboard anchor and followed the commander.

TUESDAY, MAY 20. At noon, I observed we were at [59°25'] N of latitude. At the same time, we were bearing on the southernmost part of Montague Island, which was to the N 56° W running. [We were at] 42°25' of longitude west of San Blas.

At [time omitted] in the afternoon, we were about four leagues from the coast, with the point north of Prince William Sound to the N 15°00' W and the southernmost part of Montague Island to the S 82° W. At sunrise [May 21], we saw the southernmost part of Montague Island to the S 82 W about four leagues away.

WEDNESDAY, MAY 21. At noon, I observed that we were at 59°34'N of latitude. At the same time, the southernmost part of Montague Island was at an angle of 54°01' on the quintant running. I believed the true longitude was 43°44' west of

[23]The present Middleton Island. Martínez placed them at 59°32' of latitude.

San Blas. At 7:00 P.M., the commander left in the ship's boat. At 8:15, we saw a tiny island southwest of Montague Island [which was] to the N 50° W. A high, rocky mountain range rose behind this island, which looked like the continental coast southwest of Cook's River.[24] The horizon was so clouded over, we could not see much of her. The southernmost point seen to the southwest was marked at 20°.

We crossed over and signaled to the commander about what we had seen. He answered, calling the captain to come to his ship in our boat. This was done immediately, and we faced into the wind along with the commander. At 11:00 P.M., the boat returned with the captain, who went inside and we sailed.

At sunrise [May 22], the southernmost landfall of Cook's River was to the SW 05° W. The commander put his boat in the water and an officer crossed over and came on board with an order from the commander that we should put our longboat in the water, go to the mouth formed by Montague Island and the continent, and signal him when we found good anchorage. But at 6:00, his boat returned, revoking the order. At 8:00, we sailed toward the outside with varying winds, following the commander.

THURSDAY, MAY 22. At noon, I observed that we were at 59°39' N of latitude off the southwesternmost part of Montague Island, which was at an angle of 55°01' on the quintal running. I believed we were at 43°24' of longitude, west of San Blas.

At 4:00, the boat that the commander had taken ashore arrived at his ship. At sunset, we saw the southwest point of Montague Island to the N 28° E and the southernmost point of the continental coast to the SW ¼ W. The former was about four or five leagues away. At this hour, the commander began sailing to the SW 05° S and we followed.

At dawn [May 23], we found ourselves close to land near

[24]Cook's Inlet.

the continental coast that leads to Cook's River. The islands situated at the entrance belong to Prince William Sound.[25] At sunrise, the southwesternmost part of Montague Island appeared to the N 50° E about five or six leagues away. It was impossible to see the southernmost part of the continent's coast because there was a heavy mist. At 8:15, the wind blew toward the SW ¼ and we followed the commander.

FRIDAY, MAY 23. At noon, I observed that we were at 59°42' N of latitude off the most southwestern part of Montague Island, which was to the N 50° E. I believed we were at 43°22' of longitude, west of San Blas.

At 5:00, we arrived at the entrance[26] between the southwest end of Montague Island which was to the N 24° E, an island to the N 12° E near the continent that [in part] forms the above entrance, and the southernmost end of the continent seen in the SW ¼, all about five leagues away.

SATURDAY, MAY 24. At noon, we were at 59°42' N of latitude off the southwesternmost part of Montague Island at an angle of 43°01' on the quintant. I believed the true longitude was 43°26' west of San Blas. We continued accompanied by seagulls. During my watch, we were becalmed. At 2:00 P.M., we put the launch in the water and began towing the ship toward the island. At 3:30, being more ready to sail than at two, the pilot was dispatched in a boat toward land to find a safe anchorage on the inside.

At 8:00 P.M., the wind being high, we changed direction away from the mouth and headed for the ship. At 9:00, the southwest end of Montague Island was about two leagues away to the NE ¼ E. The commander was such a long distance away that his stern was barely visible. At 11:00, the boat

[25]In 1791, Juan Francisco Bodega drew a map in San Blas which summarized Spanish discoveries on the coast up to that date for Madrid. A note on the map states: "Las Islas de Regla, which lie at La Entrada de la Rivera de Cook, were discovered and taken possession of in 1779 by Don Ignacio Arteaga and Don Juan Francisco de la Bodega y Quadra." (See: Mourelle de la Rúa, Francisco Antonio, *Voyage of the Sonora . . .*).

[26]The present Montague Strait.

arrived with the news that it had been anchored from the time it left until this hour, when the sun was cut off by clouds. For this reason, the commander fired a cannon from time to time, to which we responded.

In the morning, the southwesternmost part of Montague Island was about four leagues away to the N ¼ NE. At 4:00, we tacked NNE 09° E with good winds to the NW ¼ W. The full watch [had been spent] trying to anchor safely even if [it was] outside the mouth. At that hour, we saw the commander approaching Montague Island. At 6:00 he anchored at the southwest point.[27]

SUNDAY, MAY 25. At noon, accompanied by seagulls, we continued toward the mouth of Prince William Sound. At 7:00 P.M., the wind blew from the prow. Finding ourselves in 18 fathoms of water, we set the anchor firmly inside the southwest point of Montague Island. At this hour, we saw 11 canoes leave the land. At 7:00, they arrived, forming a line alongside the ship. The middle [canoe] carried a man who looked like a king or chief. With much singing and shouting, this chief opened his arms as if asking for peace. We answered with the same signs, encouraging him to come on board. But for the chief to get up, it was necessary for one of our men to get into one of the canoes. When he got in, he gave the Indian chief various glass beads. Then all [the Indians] began [giving us] arrows and [pieces] of bone. We did not understand why they were not surprised to see either our ship or ourselves, nor were we able to understand anything [they said], except that the island had a bay nearby. At 6:00, all 12 canoes paddled to the frigate.

At noon, I had observed that this anchorage was about 1½ leagues off the south of Montague Island at 59°49' N of latitude and 43°20' of longitude, west of San Blas.

MONDAY, MAY 26. At noon, we remained at anchor. At

[27]The present Cape Cleare.

4:00, the wind being fresh, we followed the commander in setting sail. At 7:00, we found ourselves about 4½ leagues from Prince William Sound. We anchored both ships in 17 fathoms. The southwesternmost point of Montague Island was to the S 32° E and the island's northernmost part was N 08° E. The needle remained at 59°58'N of latitude and 43°04' of longitude, west of San Blas.

TUESDAY, MAY 27. At noon, we continued toward the inside of Prince William Sound. During the afternoon, various Indian canoes came along side and one large one approached the commander's ship. Until evening, we continued navigating along the east coast of Montague Island about one mile offshore. Sighting some [smaller] islands,[28] we passed through the canal between the largest one and Montague Island. At 2:45, being nearby, the commander signaled to anchor. I believed we were at 60°08'N of latitude and 42°32' of longitude, west of San Blas.

WEDNESDAY, MAY 28. At noon, we remained anchored there, making barrels. At dawn on the 29th, the launch went ashore with the empty barrels to collect water and wood. Half of the troops were armed. Nothing else happened until 25 casks of water were collected. Four canoes of Indians came this morning and [the natives] remained on board until nightfall.

FRIDAY, MAY 30. At 5:30, both boats saluted with 11 cannons in honor of King San Fernando of Spain. We also collected eight more casks of water.

SATURDAY, MAY 31. At 10:00, the commander's boat arrived with orders for the captain and other officers to take possession of this island the next day. During the day, tar was put on the ship's sides. Four barges were built and loaded with seven casks, three barrels and wood. Near nightfall, two Indians arrived in a canoe. We tied a two-*real* coin around each of their necks with a ribbon. They left shortly afterwards.

---

[28]The *Islas Vertis* or "Green Islands" of Cook, which Martínez sighted May 26.

SUNDAY, JUNE 1. At 8:00, we went ashore in our boat with all the troops armed. The Chief Chaplain and other officers equal to the commander walked in procession along the beach with a big cross, which was already on land for this purpose. The banner of Our Lady of the Rosary was placed on top of it. When the procession was concluded, the chaplain priest Don José María Diaz said Mass. It was the first one said between 55° and 60° [of latitude] on these coasts. The chaplains of both boats, the remaining officers and the whole troop assisted. When the Mass was concluded, the cross was taken in procession to a place that had been selected close to a brook of water that ran out to the ocean, where it was separated by a great pine. The holy cross was nailed with three iron spikes to the side of the tree that faced the island's interior. Carved down its length was this inscription: *Carolus Tertius Hispaniarum & Indiarium Rex.* At the head it read: *INRI.* On the arms was carved *Año de 1788.*

During the ceremonies of the procession, Mass and procession, the soldiers fired some fusillades, each of which was answered by three cannon shots from each of the ships. Indians in five canoes watched when we came ashore, but when they heard the racket that the artillery made, they left in fear. When the function was finished, we walked the entire beach without being able to go inland because of the quantity of snow that covered the edge of the beach. But we found many blackberries, pine and cypress. We also discovered a large beam, carved by a skillful carpenter. We saw a few gray [sea] ducks with red beaks and a large number of sea gulls. The beach was covered with tiny, tiny rocks. The barges were tied to the land without a single worry. At this spot on the island, various brooks of water ran to the ocean. At the cove where we landed, we placed flowers in honor of Señor Don Manuel Antonio Flórez, Como. Viceroy of New Spain. [The place was named Port Flórez[29] after the Viceroy of New Spain.] On

[29] *Puerto de Flórez.*

this day, by order of the commander, the entrance to Prince William Sound was named the entrance of Prince Carlos [Sound].[30]

SATURDAY, JUNE 7. Today the commander and the rest of the officers held a meeting,[31] in which he proposed that, only if the winds were favorable, could we fulfill the first point that the king put in his instructions by sailing north 02°, even though there wasn't a single establishment [in the area] of Trinidad.[32] It was agreed that all of us would meet at 60°44'N of latitude, where we could see the continental shore with the

[30]By mentioning this renaming, Narváez may have been hinting at the dispute over locations that had been raging between Martínez and his officers for two weeks. According to official complaints filed by Martínez' pilot Antonio Serantes and López de Haro upon the expedition's return to San Blas, which were corroborated by Narváez and José Verdía, the conflict stemmed from a series of disputes between Martínez and Serantes over log entries. The argument began May 15, when a large island was sighted. Martínez insisted it was *Isla del Carmen* shown on the 1779 chart. Serantes said it was Cook's Montague Island, which was farther west on the chart. From then on, the infuriated Martínez allegedly treated Serantes with contempt and demanded that he alter his journal to conform with the commander's log. Among all the officers on the expedition, only Estevan Mondofía agreed with Martínez. But the commander refused to give in, prolonged the argument and resisted the urgings of his officers to fully investigate Prince William Sound.

In his report to the Viceroy on October 28, 1788, López de Haro said Martínez "reduced everything to so much foolishness...[that] from the 17th to the 23rd of May we navigated in such a disjointed fashion as Your Excellency will see in the logs, and will know that due to this defect a good many days were wasted and we lost the opportunity of entering where Captain Cook did in Prince William." [In other words, penetrating to Valdez Arm.] López de Haro alleged that Martínez ordered false courses and winds recorded to cover up his own deficiencies and his "disinclination to enter Prince William Sound."

On his chart of the voyage, López de Haro marked the *Entrada del San Carlos* at the head of Valdez Arm, which remains open-ended—i.e. unexplored.

On June 2, Martínez argued again with his officers about the expedition's position. In full view of everyone on the quarterdeck, the commander slapped Serantes, spat on him and knocked him flat. The next day, he arrested Serantes, placed him aboard the *San Carlos* as a prisoner, stripped him of all responsibilities, and replaced him with Juan Martínez y Zayas, López de Haro's second pilot. In his report to the Viceroy, Serantes said the commander's actions stemmed from "a total insanity due to drunkenness."

[31]Aboard the *Princesa.*

[32]A term Martínez first used to refer to the general area on the mainland above 61° in Prince William Sound and later gave to Cook's Trinity Islands, immediately southeast of Kodiak Island. Narvaez uses the term to refer to (in order): the mainland above 61° in Prince William Sound, the expedition's destination on Unalaska Island, and the Trinity Islands. It appears that the latter two remained confused until the *San Carlos* reached the Kenai Peninsula and the expedition obtained better information from the Russians.

naked eye. According to a report brought by the Second Pilot Don Estevan de Mondofía, who had commanded an [exploration] launch,[33] winds from the first quarter[34] would prevent us from sailing up the sound for about 10 days. If the winds did not change [and come] from below, we would then be unable to ascend to Trinidad. But if the winds were to change 02° to 03° on the quintant toward the west, we could sail up to the continent and leave through the other mouth between Montague Island and the coast.[35] Given these conditions, we all agreed and returned to our ship.[36]

TUESDAY, JUNE 10. I was ordered to sail on a fully armed launch so that I could make a survey of [Montague Island]. During the day, I navigated along the coast of Montague Island at a regular distance to the NE ¼ N. At 12:00 noon, I found myself between the northernmost part of the island and a large one named Green Island by Captain Cook.[37] From this point, I tacked NE ¼ E with a calm wind. At 6:00 P.M., I arrived at the northeasternmost point of Montague Island. But I continued to the northeast to see if I could reach the continent during the day, because I estimated we were about seven leagues from it. By 8:30, I was about four leagues away. I recognized the cove between Montague Island and the coast and the large cove called *Puerto de Santiago*[38] by the Spaniards of the past expedition.[39] This cove had been described clearly

---

[33]On June 6, Martínez had sent Mondofía in a launch to reconnoiter. He reached latitude 60°44', where he saw the continental shore.

[34]North of east.

[35]Montague Strait.

[36] Martínez recorded that it was decided to abandon any attempt to proceed farther north because of contrary winds and to go to Trinidad.

[37]*Islas Vertis* or the present Green Island.

[38]Now Port Etches on the west side of Hinchinbrook Island.

[39]In 1799. A note on a later map made by Bodgea, summarizing Spanish discoveries on North America's west coast up to 1791, states: "El Cabo de San Elías, La Montaña de San Elías, La Isla Carmen, La Ensenada de Valdés, and El Puerto de Santiago in La Isla de la Magdalena, were discovered in 1779 by Don Ignacio Arteaga and Don Francisco de la Bodega y Quadra, in which voyage [the third Bucareli expedition] possession was taken at Santiago, survey made of Los Bocas de Quadra, and also of La Isla de Quirós, now called [Isla] de Montague." (See: Mourelle de la Rúa, Francisco Antonio, *Voyage of the Sonora*. . . .)

to me by the first and second pilots of one of the ships used for the expedition of 1779.[40] They had given me various notes, which I verified.

I sailed into the cove to the ESE and found 21 fathoms of water. From there, I was pleased to see the [inlet] that Cook places at 61°[41] and a multitude of islands along the east coast of this large harbor. At 8:45, I sailed into it until I was even with Montague Island. At 10:30 P.M., I found a sheltered bridge of land and we anchored in five fathoms of water to give the crew a rest. We spent the night there.

WEDNESDAY, JUNE 11. At 3:00 A.M., I began navigating the boat. At 9:00, I arrived at a large cove about five leagues from the northwest point of Montague Island. In this cove I found about eight or 10 reefs near the middle of the island. The largest one was connected to the island. At the edge of the beach I found a large [partly destroyed house] facing the mountain.[42] The side that faced the ocean had four square windows made of wood and yellow cane. Landing the boat, I leaped ashore with the troop and saw that [the house] was intact and made with much beauty and skill. Seeing no people at all, I explored the headland a bit. I found many trees cut down with heavy axes and others with the bark removed. Some of them had been cut in the manner of shingles and placed on the top of the roof.

At 9:30 A.M., I embarked in the boat and continued sailing along the shore. At 7:15 P.M., I arrived back at the ship. During the entire expedition, I didn't encounter more than four canoes of Indians. I shared all my findings with the captain and he conveyed them to the commander.

---

[40]José Camacho and Juan Pantoja aboard the *Princesa*. They placed it at 60°14'N & 45°20'W of San Blas; it was actually 60°17'N & 41°17'W.

[41]Valdez Arm.

[42]This may have been Potap Zaikov's winter quarters in 1783-84, but the Spanish logs do not indicate they recognized it at the time as evidence of Russian presence. Later, Narváez would conclude first that it belonged to Captain Evstrat Delarov and then that it had been built by Zaikov in 1787. The mountain was Montague Peak (el. 2,175 ft.).

THURSDAY, JUNE 12. At 2:00 P.M., the launch was sent to one of the Green Islands to cut grass and wild celery. It returned at 10:00 P.M. without incident.

SUNDAY, JUNE 15. At 3:00 P.M., the commander went on watch and we started to turn at our anchorage, changing direction to the S ¼. At this hour, the wind was almost calm, so we remained in this position. After a short time, the commander cast anchor and we passed the gaskets[43] of the top mainsail.

MONDAY, JUNE 16. At 9:00, we turned at our anchorage. At 9:45, we set sail with the top mainsail and veered to the S and S ¼ SW. At 3:00, we came near the commander's ship and he sent his boat to tell us that he was going to set sail and that we should follow him. He started out, towing the ship. At 4:00, the tide was flowing through the inside and the wind was still calm, so the commander dropped anchor. We followed suit in 36 fathoms. This anchorage was between the southernmost point of Montague Island to the SSW and San Antonio Island[44] was at 38° W, each of which were about ½-mile away.

TUESDAY, JUNE 17. At 10:00 A.M., we changed direction. At 4:00 P.M., Indians [from] six canoes came on board. At 7:30, the commander dropped anchor. At 10:00, we dropped ours in 19 fathoms. We were off the southwesternmost point of Montague Island which was to the S 15° E. The most southeastern part of San Antonio Island was to the NW.

WEDNESDAY, JUNE 18. At dawn, the wind was calm but the sky gave a bad appearance. It remained that way all day. No Indians came.

Note: Two pagans that we have seen in this [region] are of moderate stature. They have light-colored skin and short,

[43]Tarred fabric wraps, which were two-to-three yards long, used to bind the furled sail to its yard.

[44]Today's La Touche and Elrington islands.

black hair. They make a hole inside their lower lip, in which they carry a carved bone with holes, from which they hang guitar-like threads of glass beads. They do the same thing with their ears. At first sight, they look like they are carrying little rattles.[45] Their bodies are covered with cloaks[46] made of skins from bears, mountain lions, and wolf-fish. Others are made of duck skin. All are carefully sewn and fitted to the body.

Their canoes are shaped like a harp and sheathed on the outside with hide perfectly sewn with little span ropes. The frames of the canoes are fabricated on the inside of very thin ribs of wood, woven into a perfectly engineered shape. In the same style, they have an enclosure in which there is a round hatch, like the mouth of an earthen jar. The Indian gets into this. No matter how much swell there is, he travels free of getting any of his body wet. His arms are free to row with small oars.

It has been noted that these pagans hold iron in high regard. They also value glass beads. On their heads, they wear perfectly woven reed hats. They smear their faces with earth that is the color of red meat. Others smudge their faces in black. They eat our food with loathing. Their food is limited to whale, marine animals and all kinds of raw fish. In place of bread they eat sliced whale. Their weapons are arrows, the heads of which are made of flint or whalebone. They use harpoons for fishing. They also carry iron daggers on some long sticks like iron-pointed staffs. They ground the iron until it is sharp and they use it for cutting things. Lacking this metal, they use flint.

With respect to their language, it is impossible to understand them. We can only make out some terms, which Captain Cook included in his vocabulary. When we repeat these,

[45] *sarrillos*.

[46] *Alba*: the alb, or long sleeved vestment worn chiefly by priests.

they continue their conversations, which remain unintelligible.

They study our ship with much attention. In the ease with which they travel along the coast, they show they have seen other expeditions. Through various signs that they repeat, they tell us that two expeditions of three-masted ships have come to this spot. We have asked them various questions about their knowledge of the Russian nation. But they answer in a manner that we do not understand. At the same time, they do not seem to understand us. In talking, it was recognized that they also are governed by a king, whom we have seen various times when he came near our ship. By the way the rest of the pagans treated him and by the things that they bartered for glass beads, we inferred that he was superior to all of them.

THURSDAY, JUNE 19. At 12:00 [noon], we sailed, fully-rigged. At 4:00 [P.M.], we found ourselves [running] E [to] W of the southernmost point of Montague Island. At 5:30, the commander anchored. At 6:30, the southwesternmost point of Montague Island was to the NE and the middle of San Antonio Island to the N 12° W, about two nautical miles away from the former.

FRIDAY, JUNE 20. At 3:45 A.M., the commander set sail and we followed at 4:30. At noon, we were at 59°50'N of latitude and the southwesternmost point of Montague Island was at an angle of 81°02' on the quintant. I believed the true longitude was 43°26' west of San Blas.

FRIDAY, JUNE 20 TO SATURDAY, JUNE 21. I could not observe our latitude because the sun was covered with clouds. The southernmost point of Montague Island was at an angle of 89°01' on the quintant and about eight or nine leagues away. I believed the true longitude was about 44°00' west of San Blas. At noon, we continued to the S ¼ SW. At 9:00 P.M., the most southeast part of Montague Island was to the N 63° E, about four leagues away.

At 2:30 A.M., we veered [toward] the pass to the ESE, which was at 05° S ¼ SW on the compass. At 3:00 A.M., the southernmost part of Montague Island was to the NE ¼ E. The southernmost part of the land was seen at 05°W, about seven leagues from the former. Nothing new happened all morning.

SATURDAY, JUNE 21 TO MIDDAY SUNDAY, JUNE 22. At sunrise, the southwestern point of Montague Island was to the N 63° E. The southernmost part of the continent could be seen to the S 55° W, about eight leagues away from the former.

SUNDAY, JUNE 22 TO MIDDAY MONDAY, JUNE 23. At noon, we remained under full sail in an effort to get near the commander, who was signaling to us from the port side that our route was contrary to the one we should follow to reach Trinidad[47] and that we should head toward the 03° of the quintant, not the 02°. At the same time, it was fortunate that he did not try to join with the packetboat in trimming sail to arrive at the same destination. He found himself lufting,[48] by which maneuver we saw [the frigate] separate itself from the packetboat.

At 7:00 P.M., the [crew] advised that they had heard cannon fire. So we immediately fired two [shots]. At 9:00 P.M., we were bearing toward the southernmost part of the continent that was visible to the WSW 05° W, about nine leagues away. At this hour we saw the commander far in the distance to the E ¼NE.

At sunrise, we were bearing toward the southernmost part of the coast which was visible to the SW ¼ W, about nine leagues away.

MONDAY, JUNE 23 TO MIDDAY TUESDAY, JUNE 24. At 2:30 A.M., a thick fog closed in. About noon, we saw the commander a long distance off the prow. It appeared that he was coming to meet us. At 3:30 P.M., we fired two cannons, in case

[47]In other words, their destination of Unalaska.

[48]*bien barbolento.*

we were getting close to him. As he did not answer, we continued firing each hour. But the commander did not answer. We continued in the direction that we believed would unite us with the commander. Sure enough, with sails trimmed, I would do this in a short time.

At 9:00 P.M., the fog dissipated and we saw the commander nearby to the ESE 05° S. This was verified by the little headway the packetboat was able to make in trying to stick to the new direction in the third quintant[49] that would take us to Trinidad. Nevertheless, we were determined to hold to this ESE course. At 10:30 P.M., we saw the Miranda Volcano[50] to the N 74° W and the southernmost part of the continent, which looked like Cape Elizabeth,[51] to the N 81° W. The latter was about 15 to 16 leagues from us.

At sunrise, a good discovery was made, and the continental land to the north was seen. At 8:00 A.M., we could not see the commander, so we all agreed to head for Trinidad[52] and wait for him there.

TUESDAY, JUNE 24 TO NOON OF WEDNESDAY, JUNE 25. At dawn, the sun was observed at 24°03' of variation NE. We saw no land. The commander has been seen from the masthead bearing to the SSE. At sunrise, we saw the commander from the mast-head off our prow, from which we inferred that he was following the same direction as we were.

WEDNESDAY, JUNE 25 TO MIDDAY THURSDAY, JUNE 26. At dawn, the sun was observed at 25°30' of variation NE. At this hour, the commander was barely distinguishable to the southwest.

THURSDAY, JUNE 26 TO MIDDAY FRIDAY, JUNE 27. At midday, I took a running compass fix on the northernmost

[49]Southwest.

[50]*Volcan de Miranda* or the present Iliamna Volcano (elevation 10,016 feet) in the Aleutian Range. Previously sighted by Arteaga and Bodega in 1779.

[51]*Cabo Elizavel,* the southeastern tip of the Kenai Peninsula at 59°09'of latitude and 151°03' west of Greenwich.

[52]In other words, the expedition's destination—Unalaska Island.

part of Cape Grenville[53] to the N 06° E. I observed that we were at 57°N of latitude. I believed our longitude was 47°16' west of San Blas. I believed that Trinidad Island[54] was bearing to the WSW, about three leagues away.

At 8:00 P.M., we took in the upper studding sails[55] and the mainsail. We took a sounding and found ourselves in 35 fathoms of water. At 10:00, we sounded in 45 fathoms of water, sandy bottom.

At 6:00 A.M. [June 27], we sounded again in 45 fathoms of water. The sky cleared and we saw land to the southwest. At 10:00 A.M., we sounded in three fathoms, rocky bottom. During a short period of fine weather, the land was seen clearly at Cape Grenville, which had two points—the western one was to the N 26° W and the eastern one was to the N 19° E.

FRIDAY, JUNE 27 TO NOON SATURDAY, JUNE 28. At noon, I could not take a sighting because the sun was covered with clouds.[56] The Cape of Two Points[57] appeared to the west at an angle of 68°04' on the quintant, about four leagues away. I estimated we were at 57°07'N of latitude and 48°09' of longitude, west of San Blas and that Trinidad Island[58] was to the SW ¼ W, about 18 leagues away.

At 3:45 P.M., we sounded in 81 fathoms, fine sand bottom. At 4:00, we headed SSE. At 9:00 P.M., it cleared up and I took a running fix on the coast, which was seen about nine leagues away. I saw Cape Grenville to the NNE 07° E and the Cape of Two Points to the [W] 10° N.

---

[53]Today's Cape Chiniak, the northeasternmost point of Kodiak Island.

[54]Actually the present Trinity Islands: Tugidak Island and Sitkinak Island(s), which Narváez then thought were Unalaska Island.

[55]A narrow sail set on a boom extending outwards from the end of the yard carrying a square sail.

[56]Here the North Pacific low-pressure systems collide; days are overcast more than half the year, often with pea-soup visibility or howling 60-knot gales.

[57]A cape called *Cabo de dos Puntos* by López de Haro, who recorded sighting a wall of rock to the west between two points. Probably Cook's "Two-Headed Point" and today's Sitkalidak Island.

[58]In other words, the Trinity Islands, which he thought were Unalaska Island.

At 3:30 A.M., Cape Grenville bore to the N ¼ NE and the Cape of Two Points was to the W ¼ SW, about four leagues from the former. At 4:30 A.M., 12 canoes of Indians came out of a large bay located to the [western] side of the Cape of Two Points. After they came aboard, we gave them ribbons and beads. We noted that these Indians had been trading with some civilized nation. One Indian approximated saluting with his hat. Another took out an ordinary wooden box full of tobacco-like snuff and, after taking a drink, he wanted us to drink with him. He also took out a slip of paper written in English or Russian and dated 1784, so that we could read it to them. Afterwards, he anxiously asked for us to return it. We attempted to ingratiate ourselves with him by giving him another piece of paper written by us, so that he would leave the first one with us. That's how we actually got it.[59]

At 9:00 A.M., the Indians went ashore. At 10:00 A.M., we sounded in 53 fathoms, white sand and shells.

SATURDAY, JUNE 28 AT MIDDAY TO SUNDAY, JUNE 29. At noon, it was impossible to take a sighting because the sun was covered. I took a running fix on the Cape of Two Points to the N 08° W. It was about five leagues away. I estimated we were at 56°50' N of latitude and 48°30' of longitude, west of San Blas, with Trinidad Island to the W ¼ SW, about 14 leagues away.

---

[59]According to López de Haro, the natives carried several small scraps of paper bearing Russian writing. He got the impression these were vouchers for payment of tribute. He exchanged trinkets for five of the bills. The bills were eventually turned over to the Viceroy. These or similar ones now reside in the Spanish National Archives. (See: Cook, Warren, *Flood Tide of Empire*, p. 124 and fn. 93.)

Note: Between June 29 and July 1, Martínez engaged in a similar exchange. To obtain tribute slips from the natives, he made out new receipts in Spanish which said: "This person presented me with a slip of paper dated 1786. The Spanish expedition belongs to his Catholic Majesty, the King of Spain, Don Carlos III, God Keep Him, then anchored on this island on June 27th, 1788. The commander is Esteban José Martínez." He then initialed the receipts and gave them to the Indians. See: *Diario de Esteban José Martínez*, June 29-July 1, 1788 and *Diario de Antonio Palacios*, June 29-30, 1788. Note: Until now, historians have only given Martínez credit for cleverly obtaining this important evidence of the Russian's presence. See Inglis, Robin, *Spain and the North Pacific Coast*, p. 14.

At 7:00 P.M., we sounded at 85 fathoms, fine black sand. Three canoes of Indians arrived and came aboard. They indicated with hand signs that they had ships in the large bay[60] on the [west] side of the Cape of Two Points. At sunset, the bay was SW, about three leagues away.

At sunrise, the Cape of Two Points was to the S 75° W, about three leagues away. We were in 43 fathoms, dark sand bottom with some rock and small shells.

SUNDAY, JUNE 29 AT MIDDAY TO MONDAY, JUNE 30. At noon, we continued SSW toward Trinidad Island under full sail. At 12:30 P.M., we were about four leagues from the mouth of the bay to the west of the Cape of Two Points. Two canoes of Indians arrived and came aboard. They were dressed in blue shirts, shoes and stockings. We gave them beads and asked who had given them their clothes. Using hand signals, they told us that there were people living on the bay's shore who were like us and that they had two ships. To verify this information, we immediately decided to go to the bay and reconnoiter so we could find out if the information the Indians had given us between Cape Grenville and this cape was true.

At 1:00 P.M., we sounded in 46 fathoms, coarse gravel. At 2:30, we were in 17 fathoms, same bottom. At 2:45, we were in 15 fathoms, same bottom. We hauled in the sail and dropped anchor about one league from the Cape of Two Points. We launched one boat and prepared to sail as soon as the fog cleared. From this anchorage, the cape's [western] point was to the N 37° W and the eastern point was to the N 17° E. The end of the bay where the Russians were believed to have an establishment was to the NW 05° W. An island[61] lay to the S 47° W of this bay, about two nautical miles from the mainland. Trinidad Island was to the S 26° W.

MONDAY, JUNE 30 AT NOON TO TUESDAY, JULY 1. At 3:00 A.M., the captain assigned me to go in the launch armed

[60]The entrance to the present Sitkalidak Strait.

[61]Probably the present Two Headed Island.

for war to reconnoiter the bay. I headed toward the Cape's [western] point. At 5:00 A.M., we entered the bay between that point and a small reef to the [east].[62] As the bay opened to the east, I saw seven three-man canoes coming out. So I immediately went over to them to see if I could obtain some information. Once we were among them, I saw that four Russians rode in four of the canoes. They seemed cautious about coming along side. I greeted them and they answered. Using signs, I asked if they wanted to come aboard the packetboat and they answered affirmatively. So we returned directly to the ship, where they stayed until 3:00 P.M.

During our discourse,[63] we were able to obtain the following information. We asked them what nation they were from and they told us they were Russians. When we unfolded our Spanish insignias, they asked if we were Spanish, and we answered affirmatively. We explained that a flag we had carved in wood was the latest one used by Spain since early in 1786.

One of them was the commandant of the village. His name was Captain Del Aro.[64] The other three officers didn't seem to know how to communicate in any language except Russian. We were as cordial as possible, which enabled us to acquire considerable information. By putting various questions to the captain by signs and by writing, we learned he was a Greek, born in Constantinople, and the other three officers were from Siberia. The captain had been at this outpost since November 2, 1787. The other three officers had been there from the first part of 1784. They intended to remain until 1790, when they would be resupplied by two frigates from Siberia.[65]

---

[62]The bay became known as Three Saints Bay.

[63]As Mondofía was the only member of the expedition who spoke any Russian and he was on the *Princesa,* Narváez and López de Haro were forced to use sign language.

[64]Evstrat (Eustrate) Delarov, whose name sounded very similar to "de Haro" to the Spaniards. In 1789, Delarov was named head of the Shelikhov-Golikov Company in America.

[65]According to López de Haro, Delarov said the expedition would occupy Nootka Sound, where sea otters were known to be abundant.

We stopped our inquires for a few hours because we didn't want them to get the impression we were unusually curious about their situation. After eating, they asked if we had seen a galliot[66] in Prince William Sound. We said that we had seen the ship[67] and a house on the east side of Montague Island. The [Russian] captain said that the galliot and the house were his and that he had another house at 61°. The former [house] was the one that I saw when I went out to reconnoiter that area.

We were eager to obtain as much information as possible from this valuable source. Using his discretion, Captain [López de Haro] gave the Russians a barrel of wine, some chocolate and other things to get them to tell us more. The one who was most appreciative invited us to come to their establishment inside the port.

We accepted the invitation and pulled out our chart of these coasts to see if they would either point out some other establishments or give another name to the Port of Nootka or Prince William Sound. When Captain Del Aro saw it, he took a pencil and drew a very wide and navigable canal, which began south of Cook's River[68] and extended to Trinidad Island, making all that large portion of what we thought was the continental coast an island.[69] This was most useful information, because Cook did not show [the strait] on his chart. So we asked if he had a chart we could see. [Captain Del Aro] told us he would give us a chart when we came ashore.

At 3:00 P.M., they asked us to take them ashore. Captain [López de Haro] immediately ordered us to man the launch and he asked me to transport [the Russians] to their establish-

---

[66]Sloop.

[67]Narváez did not mention seeing a Russian ship in Prince William Sound. His entry for June 18 refers to Indians reporting two earlier expeditions of three-masted ships.

[68]Cook's Inlet.

[69]Delarov drew Shelikof Strait, west of Kodiak. Up to that time, the Spaniards thought Kodiak was part of the mainland. They must have also realized that their destination of "Trinidad Island" was much further away than they had anticipated.

ment so that I could find out where it was located. In a little spot that was well protected and hidden, they had built a village of about five wooden houses. Some of them were large. In front of the trader's houses near the beach, they had hauled up two de-masted galliots[70] of about 80 tons burden each. When I asked the captain why he had beached the ships, he led me to believe they were intended as a fortress to guard against attacks by Indians. On top of the house behind these ships they had built a round fortified tower made of wood. In this tower a Russian sentinel was posted. I did not see any artillery other than four or five small stone mortars in each ship. But I did see some big flashes from small cannons, because they saluted me when I left. As I approached land, about 40 or 50 Russians and a multitude of domesticated Indians came out to the beach. They had another small, two-masted schooner anchored on the beach.

As soon as they gave me the chart of the area between Cape Elizabeth and Trinidad Island,[71] which the captain had promised, I sheered off and sailed along the coast of the bay. I saw small forts along the beach at regular intervals. We learned later that they were lookouts. I also saw two Indian villages, one of which was very large, located on the bay's eastern shore. At 11:30 P.M., I returned to the ship and reported my findings to Captain [López de Haro].

TUESDAY, JULY 1. At 7:00 P.M., the captain sailed in the launch armed for war to the [Russian] establishment, with the aim of finding out whatever he could. At 8:00, a canoe with 20 Russians arrived loaded with fish, which they gave to us. We welcomed them aboard and gave them in return liquor and other trifles, which they [welcomed].

At about that time, another canoe arrived with two Indians. One of them entered the cabin looking very serious. He

[70]Swift coastal merchant ships; galleys.

[71]In other words, between the southeastern tip of the Kenai Peninsula and Unalaska Island.

handed a written message to one of the Russians, who seemed superior to the others. After he read it, he told me through signs that the day before a Spanish frigate had anchored at the Trinity Islands.[72] When I asked who had sent the message, he told me that it had come from a Russian lookout stationed on one of those islands. All the visitors left in a short while.

At 9:00 P.M., the launch arrived carrying Captain [López de Haro] and one of the Russians who had visited the previous day. The captain gave us the following information.

When he landed, Captain Del Aro and other officers had come out to receive him. He noticed that the Russians had two small gardens, in which they grew various vegetables. From there they took him to see a huge warehouse, made of two parts, that they were just finishing constructing. They also showed him a house in which they had a school, filled with many Indians of different ages, to whom they were teaching reading, writing and the catechism in the Russian language. Boarding one of the galliots that they had beached, the captain saw a chapel in one of them where they said Mass. Captain [Del Aro] also lived in this ship. In the other one, they had a watchtower with a soldier standing guard. An officer also lived there. The ships were placed there to intimidate the Indians and to store the otter skins that they collected. Both were nearly full. They call the two-masted ships galliots. They are each of about 80 tons burden. They carry a single cannon and four small stone mortars.

Other than the pistols and side arms carried by each Russian, these are the only weapons that [Captain López de Haro] saw. Later, he was taken to a huge house in which there were many Indians. Ten cauldrons were set on the fire. Some were used to boil whale oil, others for frying fish, and others for smoking fish. These were winter provisions.

Then they took [Captain López de Haro] to a large enclo-

---

[72] *Islas de Trinidad* or the present Trinity Islands, due south of Kodiak Island. Narváez and López de Haro naturally concluded it was the *Princesa*.

sure, in which they kept many otter skins set out to dry. They placed one skin in his hands and told him that it had a great deal of value in China. Then they took him to a house of one of the officers who had come aboard. He was acting as storehouse guard. The captain learned that this man was married to a good-looking woman dressed in the same style as the Chinese, with very good clothes of silk. At the same time he saw two more women dressed in the same style. When he asked Captain [Del Aro] where the women came from, he was told they were daughters of Siberia.

The houses of this officer and the captain were large but low. They were made of boards with various partitions for the rest of the Russians. The roofs were covered with grass. The apartment of the captain and officer were attractively adorned with wallpaper painted in China, a large mirror and a few framed pictures of saints. At one end of the apartment was an iron woodstove, about 12 inches square and 33 inches high.

All the Indians were dressed in wolf or skunk skins, except for the ones who had become Christians.[73] These people wore short clothes of corduroy and boots, like the rest of the Russians. The Russians had trained these Indians well. A Russian only had to speak once and all the Indians came quickly to see what was being asked of them. The Russian captain told ours to beware of Indians along the coast because they were considered treacherous. This appeared true, because many Russians were seen with arrow wounds received in a recent major skirmish.

At 2:00 P.M., Captain Del Aro retired to his apartment, where [Captain López de Haro] asked if the Russians had a village on Trinity Island. The Russian said they only had a watchtower there, but they had a total of 462 Russians at Cook's River, Unalaska Island and other places on the coast.[74] [Captain López de Haro] also asked if the Russians had an

[73]Mainly somewhat acculturated Aleut hunters.

[74]By exaggerating his manpower at 462, the wily Delarov was probably trying to bluff the Spaniards out of getting interested in Nootka.

establishment at Prince William [Sound]. [Captain Del Aro] said no, but he expected two frigates to come from Siberia during the coming year to populate this location.

At 3:00 P.M., [Captain López de Haro] took his leave from Captain Del Aro and the other officers and returned to our ship. On the way, he was accompanied by the officer who guarded the warehouse. At 5:30 P.M., the captain arrived in the launch, carrying the Russian.

At 7:00 P.M., the Russian captain arrived in a canoe that had come from the establishment. He showed us a chart and a royal dispatch that he had just received from Cape Elizabeth. The dispatch was written in Russian, but an attached letter appeared to be written in English. Thinking it was written in our language, he gave it to us so we could read it to him. He said the dispatch said the letter was delivered by a captain of a frigate that had just anchored in Cook's River.[75] Seeing that I did not understand the letter, he read the dispatch to the other Russian who was on board. But he remained confused and bewildered.

We were only able to copy the letter and the chart. Using sign language, we asked how many Russians they had at all of the villages on the coast. The captain repeated the figure of 462. He asked for the chart of these coasts so he could show us the outposts. As soon as we handed it to him, he gave the following explanation.

First, he pointed to his establishment [at Three Saints Bay] and said there were 60 Russians and two galliots. He made some calculations on a piece of paper. Then he pointed to another outpost west of Cape Elizabeth, where he numbered 40 Russians. He pointed to another at Cape Rada[76] and num-

[75]The copied letter was eventually turned over to the Viceroy. It now resides in the Spanish National Archives. The letter from William Douglas to Horeman Sycoff (i.e. Potap Zaikov) is dated June 25, 1788 at Cook's River.(See: Cook, Warren, *Flood Tide of Empire*, p. 124 and fn. 93.)

[76]A "cape" south of Cape Elizabeth, which Martínez called *Cabo de Rada*. On López de Haro's chart, it is shown clearly as an island opposite Cape Douglas on the mainland. It was probably today's Afognak Island.

bered 37 Russians. He pointed to another on the mainland at Cook's Inlet at 58°18' of latitude and 205°15' of longitude, west of Greenwich and he numbered 40 Russians. Inside Cook's River, he said there were 70 Russians and a galliot. On the mainland at 55°15' latitude and 198°37' of longitude west of Greenwich, he pointed to another village with 55 Russians and a galliot. On Unalaska Island, he pointed to another village with 120 Russians and two galliots. Then he pointed to a house on the east side of Montague Island and another at 61° of latitude, at which he said there were 40 Russians and a galliot. He said each summer these men roamed the Coast as far as Nootka Sound collecting furs, which they stored in the second building. In the winter, they retired to their village.

After [Captain Del Aro] finished explaining all of this, he added up all the entries noted on his paper and it resulted in the same 462 men that he had estimated earlier. We considered ourselves fully informed about all the Russian establishments. At 11:00, the Russian captain returned to his village and the other officer slept on board our ship.

WEDNESDAY, JULY 2. At 9:45 A.M., we left under full sail with the aim of rendezvousing with the commander at his reported anchorage at Trinidad Island.[77] At 11:00, the Russian official who had slept on board the night before left. At noon, the [western] point of the Cape of Two Points was to the NW, about three leagues away.

WEDNESDAY, JULY 2 AT MIDDAY TO NOON THURSDAY, JULY 3. At midday, we continued under full sail. At 8:00 P.M., the [western] point of the Cape of Two Points was to the N 57° W and the [westernmost] part of the island was seen to the W 06° S, about eight or nine leagues away from the former. Neither Trinidad Island nor the headland were visible, because there was a large amount of fog.

At 3:30 A.M., the [western] point of the Cape of Two Points

[77]The Trinity Islands, directly southeast of Kodiak Island.

was to the N 30° W and Trinidad Island was to the S 25° W, about four leagues from the former. At 8:00 A.M., we saw the frigate anchored to the north and east of Trinidad Island. She flew her insignias and we raised our flag. At noon, I was unable to make an observation, because the sun was covered and the anchorage was only two leagues away.

THURSDAY, JULY 3 AT MIDDAY TO FRIDAY, JULY 4. We continued under full sail toward the anchorage. At 1:30 P.M., being near the frigate, we saluted with six large cannon shots. [The commander's] ship responded with three. At 2:30, we dropped our starboard anchor in 33 fathoms alongside the commander. We furled all sails and then sent the commander a report of the information we had obtained.

That anchorage was southeast of the easternmost end of Trinidad Island.[78] One ridge of rocks emerged from the point to the SE ¼ E. The most northwesterly part of the island was to the S 64° W. Trinidad ran due west and the Cape of Two Points was to the N 02° E.

At 5:00 P.M., the commander's launch arrived with an order for the captain. At 8:00 P.M., the launch returned with his reply.[79]

FRIDAY, JULY 4 AT NOON TO SATURDAY, JULY 5. On this island we have seen some very large differences with each ebb tide, which took 6½ to seven hours. No Indians came aboard during the day. But the commander had learned that a Russian, accompanied by two or three Indians, lived here. This morning the commander sent an order for the captain.

SATURDAY, JULY 5 AT NOON TO SUNDAY, JULY 6. At 11:00 A.M., the commander set sail and we followed. At 5:00 P.M., the commander signaled for us to anchor. Both ships anchored in 46 fathoms. The northeast end of Trinidad Island was to the W 04° S and the southwestern part was to the SW 03° W, both about two leagues away. At 2:00 A.M., the com-

[78]Apparently, Sitkinak Island. [79]Literally, *contestación*, or answering arguments.

mander set sail and we followed. At noon, we were at 56°15'N of latitude, with the southern end of Trinidad Island 25°NE. I believed we were at 49°30' of longitude, west of San Blas.

SUNDAY, JULY 6 AT MIDDAY TO MONDAY, JULY 7. At noon, we were at 55°42' of latitude and the southeastern part of Foggy Island was three leagues to the [west]. I estimated the longitude was 51° west of San Blas. I noted that the islands Cook placed there were not heeling to the [west] at WSW 05° S, 32 leagues away.

At midday, we continued southwest under full sail. At 8:00 P.M., the Foggy Islands came into sight and we signaled to the commander about the one to the southwest. At sunset, we saw the southeastern part of Trinidad Island to the N 12° E and the center of the Foggy Islands to the S 43° W. The two islands were about 13 leagues away from each other.

At sunrise, we saw the Foggy Islands to the southwest about 4.5 to 5 leagues away. At 12:00 noon, we realized it was only one long island, shaped like a half moon, with its bosom facing north.[80]

MONDAY, JULY 7 AT NOON TO TUESDAY, JULY 8. At sunrise, the southeastern part of Foggy Island was to the N 07° E, about six leagues away. At 10:30, we lost sight of the commander. The night was somewhat dark.

TUESDAY, JULY 8 AT NOON TO WEDNESDAY, JULY 9. At noon, we continued without incident. Because of a thick fog, we lost sight of the commander.

WEDNESDAY, JULY 9 AT NOON TO THURSDAY, JULY 10. At midday, I observed that we were at 54°27' N of latitude and the southwest of the islands that Captain Cook discovered in that area of the east[81] were to the N 10° E. By my estimate, we were at 54°47' of longitude west of San Blas. I estimated that Unalaska Island was about 72 leagues away at an angle of 85°03' on the quintant.

[80]It was probably today's Chirikof Island, named *Infante* by Martínez.

[81]Martínez states that on this day he sighted Cook's Shumagin Islands, counted 33 of them and named them *Islas de los Pilotos*.

At 5:00 P.M., the commander signaled to us about land off the starboard bow, which we marked to the E 05° N. It appeared to be islands that [Cook] placed farther east. At 8:30, the eastern side of one of these islands was to the N 70° W and the eastern side of the other was to the N 30° W, and both were about six leagues away. At this hour, the sun was at 19°37' of variation NE. At dawn, the [westernmost] part of the islands were to the NW ¼ W, with the most easterly one to the N 03° E, about seven or eight leagues away.

THURSDAY, JULY 10 AT NOON TO FRIDAY, JULY 11. As it was very foggy, both ships fired cannon shots throughout the night to remain in contact.

FRIDAY, JULY 11 AT NOON TO SATURDAY, JULY 12. At noon, we continued under full sail, returning WSW. At 6:45 P.M., we sounded in 42 fathoms, with a bottom of fine black sand and small coarse gravel. At 7:15 P.M., I sounded in 38 fathoms, with the same bottom. At 8:00, the fog cleared a bit and we saw Rodiac Island[82] clearly from this anchorage. The southwest part of the island was to the N 73° W and the southeast part was to the N 47° W, about four leagues away.

SATURDAY, JULY 12 AT NOON TO SUNDAY, JULY 13. At noon, we remained anchored along with the commander. At 1:00 P.M., we wound in the anchor. As it was hoisted, we saw that it came up without the anchor-stock, so we stayed close to the commander. At 4:30 P.M., the anchor was ready with another stock and [it was] on the cable. At this time, a man fell overboard. We immediately hauled up the mainsail and lay to with the main-topsail to the front and we were able to pick him up.

At 8:30 P.M., we saw an island that was to the N 57° W, about five leagues away. At 9:30 P.M., we dropped anchor in 36 fathoms. At 3:45 A.M., it cleared up a bit and we saw Rodiac Island[83] about three leagues away.[84] The commander anchored about one league to windward.

---

[82]Named *Zayas ó Plies* by Martínez, it is the present Sanak Islands.

[83]The present Sanak Islands.

[84]López de Haro placed it at 54°03' of latitude and 56°58' longitude, west of San Blas.

SUNDAY, JULY 13 AT NOON TO MONDAY JULY 14. At noon, we remained anchored. At 6:00 P.M., we saw: to the N ¼ NW, that part of the coast marked Cape Alvides;[85] to the N 85° W, the southwestern part of Rodiac Island; to the N 80° W and southeast of Rodiac, the eastern part of a thin little isle that was about two nautical miles long. We were about five leagues from the large island and about four leagues from the little one. At noon, I could not observe the sun's location because it was overcast.

MONDAY, JULY 14 TO TUESDAY, JULY 15. At noon, I could not observe the sun's location because it was covered by cloud. We marked Rodiac Island about four leagues away to the N 33° W[86] running and at 57°13' of longitude west of San Blas. Unalaska Island was 20 leagues away to the W 06° S.[87] At dawn, we saw the continental coast laden with snow.

TUESDAY, JULY 15 AT NOON TO WEDNESDAY, JULY 16. At noon, we continued fully rigged. At sunset, the southwest part of Rodiac Island was to the NW ¼ N, about six leagues away. At dawn, we saw a point of land jutting toward the northwest of the W ¼ NW, about 14 leagues away. It was the large island that lies to the southwest of the cape[88] at which Cook placed an island. To avoid confusion in the markings, we named it San Gonzalo.[89] At 7:00 A.M., it was being covered with fog. In the middle of it, we saw a high [sharp mountain][90] to the N 40° W, about 14 leagues away. At 12:00 noon, not seeing the commander, we tacked to the WSW to come along side the island.

WEDNESDAY, JULY 16 AT MIDDAY TO THURSDAY, JULY 17. At midday, we continued under full sail without seeing the frigate. At sunset, we saw it off the port side anchor. It seemed

---

[85]Left unmarked by the expedition; possibly Cape Pankof.

[86]Narváez omits the latitude. López de Haro estimated 54°07'.

[87]López de Haro estimated it was 39.5 leagues distant.

[88]The "Rocks of Cook" or Cape Pankof.

[89]The present Unimak Island.

[90]Shishaldin Volcano, elevation 9,372 ft., named *Fernandez* by Martínez.

to be following the same course as we were. At 12:00 midnight, we sounded in 50 fathoms. At sunrise, we were encouraged by seeing the commander about three leagues away to the southwest and discovering he was following the same tack as we are. At 12:00 noon, we saw the land to the northeast of Unalaska Island and sounded in 40 fathoms.

Note: Based on dead reckoning, I estimated that Unalaska Island was about 21 leagues to the WSW. But it gradually cleared up and by midday we saw island reefs or sharp points of land that reached towards us from the northeast. They seem to be the islands that are northeast of Unalaska. At noon, we were at 53°56' of latitude, but I didn't count it as a good observation because I caught the sun at 12:00 without having seen it rise. I give more credit to it as an estimate. There was no other novelty, except the fact that we hit a horrible current.

THURSDAY, JULY 17 AT MIDDAY TO FRIDAY, JULY 18. At noon, I could not make an observation because the sun was covered. We were southwest of the first big island that is east of Unalaska,[91] which was about three leagues away. I estimated we were at 54°08' latitude and at 59°39' of longitude, west of San Blas. At noon, we tacked to the west, with Unalaska Island about one league away to the WSW.[92] At 7:00 P.M., we sounded in 50 fathoms. At midnight, we sounded in 41 fathoms. At 2:00 A.M., we sounded in 33 fathoms. At 5:00 A.M., it cleared up a bit and we saw what appeared to be even more islands off the prow. So we believed we were farther north than we had thought. We headed southwest along the shore for 1½ leagues in 38 fathoms of water.

FRIDAY, JULY 18 AT NOON TO SATURDAY, JULY 19. At noon, we were at 53°51'N of latitude. At the same time, I took a running fix on Cape Providence[93] at an angle of 58°03'E on

[91]Tigalda Island or Sedanka Island?

[92]López de Haro said Cape Providencia [Biorka] was five leagues south at 50°WSW.

[93]The present Cape Biorka?

the quintant, so I estimated we were at 60°15' of longitude west of San Blas. We remained about five leagues away from the cape in a narrow strait[94] between the island and some reefs. We continued under full sail.

At 2:00 P.M., we sounded in 45 fathoms. At 4:00, the wind blew to the northeast and we continued sailing south in 40 to 45 fathoms of water along the coast of the chain of islands, which were about three-quarters of a league away. At 7:30, we sighted another island that looked like the last one [in the chain][95] and a strip of land to the southwest from Unalaska Island. At 9:30, we sounded in 46 fathoms. At midnight, we were in 48 fathoms. At 4:00 A.M., Unalaska Island was seen off the prow. So we tacked toward the W ¼ SW in the canal between Cape Providence[96] on Unalaska to the S 90° W and the eastern point of the big island[97] to the W 05° N, about five leagues away from the former. The [string of] islands[98] that we had passed was about 14 leagues long. At 8:00, we saw the commander following the same course. But we were unable to reunite because the frigate went faster. At 11:30, we could not see the commander. We believed he probably anchored in one of the bays or canals among the islands.[99]

SATURDAY, JULY 19 AT MIDDAY TO SUNDAY, JULY 20. At noon, I took a running fix on Cape Providence to the southwest. By my estimate, we were at [an unrecorded position] of latitude and 60°25' of longitude, west of San Blas. The mouth of the canal's entrance was to the [W] 07° N. At noon, we continued under full sail. At 4:00 P.M., we continued [west]

[94]Akutan Pass, between Unalaska and Akutan.

[95]Akutan Island.

[96]On Capt. Cook's chart, Cape Providence is marked at the northeast tip of the present Sedanka Island, where Biorka is now located.

[97]Akutan.

[98]The present Krenitzin Islands.

[99]Again, the two ships lost contact. They would remain out of communication for 11 days and would not reunite for 17 days. On the 21st, Martínez landed at a bay on the northwest side of Unalaska Island, which he named *Princesa de Asturias,* and took possession. On July 29, he went ashore at Unalaska Inlet.

through the canal along the coast of the last island at a distance of about one league. At this hour, we sounded in 44 fathoms. At 6:30, we sounded in 33 fathoms. From this anchorage, there was a pass to the SSW and the southwestern part of the island where we had anchored, which is the one that with Unalaska Island forms a canal to the W 04° S, about five nautical miles away.

SUNDAY, JULY 20 AT NOON TO MONDAY, JULY 21. At noon, we were at 53°54'N of latitude and Cape Providence was to the SW ¼ W running. So I estimated we were at 60°35' of longitude, west of San Blas. We were about 5½ leagues from the canal's entrance, which was to the NW ¼ W.

At 3:30 P.M., we sounded in 45 fathoms and anchored in 46 fathoms. This anchorage was about four leagues away from Cape Providence, which was to the SW ¼ W.

MONDAY, JULY 21 AT NOON TO TUESDAY, JULY 22. At midday, I could not make an observation because the sun was covered. The compass indicated that Cape Providence was to the WSW 05° S running, and about three leagues away. By my estimate, we were at 60°16' of longitude west of San Blas. We were about 3½ leagues away from the canal's eastern point, which was to the NW. At 8:00 P.M., Cape Providence was to the S 30° W, about four leagues away.

TUESDAY, JULY 22 AT NOON TO WEDNESDAY, JULY 23. At noon, I could not make an observation because the sun was covered. By the compass, Cape Providence was at 32°03' on the quintant and about 3½ leagues away from the islands. By my estimate, we were at 53°54'N of latitude and 60°13' of longitude, west of San Blas. The mouth of the canal was to the W ¼ W, about five leagues away.

At 6:00 P.M., we were in 56 fathoms of water. At 8:00 P.M., the northeast part of Unalaska Island was to the N 04° W and the eastern entrance of the canal was to the SW ¼ W. The coast was about three leagues away. At sunrise, Cape Providence was to the SW ¼ W and the mouth of the canal was to the SW ¼ W. The closest part of the land was unclear to the NW, about three leagues away.

WEDNESDAY, JULY 23 AT NOON TO THURSDAY, JULY 24. At noon, we were at 53°35'N of latitude, opposite the middle of the northernmost island in the chain of islands that ran NW. By my estimate, we were at 60° of longitude, west of San Blas. The mouth of the canal was to the NW, about 12 leagues away.

At 6:00 A.M., we saw land about five leagues away during a brief clearing but we were unable to mark it. At 12:00 noon, the sky cleared and I was able to mark this land well.

THURSDAY, JULY 24 AT NOON TO FRIDAY, JULY 25. At noon, we were at 53°38'N of latitude and I took a running fix on Cape Providence to the W ¼ NW. By my estimate, we were at 60°13' of longitude, west of San Blas. The mouth of the canal was to the NW 03° W, about 14 leagues away.

At sunset, the northeasternmost island was to the N 37° W and the southwesternmost one was to the N 67° W, both about eight leagues away.

FRIDAY, JULY 25 AT MIDDAY TO SATURDAY, JULY 26. At sunset, the southwesternmost end of Unalaska Island was to the S 61° W, the most northerly islets were to the NE ¼ N and the canal's mouth was to the S 62° W. The last one was about three leagues away. From the time it got dark until 9:30 P.M., we were in 52 fathoms of water. At 9:30, the northeasternmost part of Unalaska Island was at NW 05° W running, about 1½ leagues away.

At 7:00 A.M., we sounded in 60 fathoms. At 9:00, we were in 59 fathoms. At 12:00 noon, we were in 68 fathoms. It remained so foggy that we could not see land.

SATURDAY, JULY 26 AT MIDDAY TO SUNDAY, JULY 27. We continued to be unable to see land because of the fog, but we believed we were very close to it. At 4:00 P.M., we sounded in

44 fathoms; at 6:00 in 35 fathoms. So I decided to drop anchor and stay in this position until the fog lifted, because it was impossible to know our true situation. The ship was driven by strong currents, which we were unable to predict. Some ran east and others to the west and the force depended on where we were located. At 6:30 P.M., we dropped our starboard anchor. We experienced nothing unusual, except the silence of the night and the noise of waves on the beach. At dawn, the fog was still heavy and it stayed that way until midday.

SUNDAY, JULY 27 TO NOON ON MONDAY, JULY 28. At noon, we were still anchored in calm water and surrounded by heavy fog all day. At 2:30 A.M., it cleared a bit at 04° on the quintant and we saw land about 1½ nautical miles away. It was impossible to get a clear compass reading, but we knew we were anchored next to the islet that forms a canal with Unalaska Island. Almost immediately, the fog closed in again and stayed until 10:00 A.M. Then it cleared again and I was able to make compass readings. Cape Providence was to the SW. The northeasternmost land that was seen to the N 60° E—which is the second little island and a medium-sized one of the canal—formed a canal with Unalaska Island to the SSW, and that's where we were anchored. From 10:00 to midday, we fired our large cannons to see if either the commander would answer or Indians would approach.

MONDAY, JULY 28 AT NOON TO TUESDAY, JULY 29. At noon, we remained at anchor in calm water. The current flowed with great force toward the [west]. At nightfall, the sky was clear. During the night, the weather continued to improve until it got clear and beautiful. At 9:00 A.M., we put the longboat in the water so that we could either sail it through the inside or use it as a tow.

TUESDAY, JULY 29 AT NOON TO WEDNESDAY, JULY 30. At 1:30 P.M., three canoes of Indians arrived. One of them carried a Russian, who came from the village of Unalaska. He brought two letters for Captain [López de Haro] from the commander, who was anchored inside a bay where the Russians had an establishment. The bay[100] was [west] of the canal. The captain answered immediately, sending his letter with two of the Indians. The Russian and three Indians remained on board to direct us to the village.

At 6:00 P.M., we weighed anchor and set out, towing the ship by the prow with the longboat. A huge current carried us out into the canal.

WEDNESDAY, JULY 30 AT MIDDAY TO THURSDAY, JULY 31. At 3:00 P.M., we were [moving from] north [to] south in the mouth, heading for Unalaska. At 6:30 P.M., we were in 40 fathoms of water and the current was hitting us too much in the stern and driving us to the [west]. We pulled down all sail and dropped our starboard anchor. We saw no land because the fog was so thick. But we believed this spot was encircled by land and close to the island that was at the north end of the canal.

At dawn, it was calm and clear. At sunrise, we saw the southernmost point of the island that was north of the mouth of Unalaska Inlet, which had two rocks at S 85° E. We also saw the easternmost part of Unalaska Island at S 50° E of this point. Behind it was the canal, in the middle of which were two very small reefs that were connected to Unalaska Island. These formed the canal's straits. The mouth of the Unalaska Inlet was S 20° E. It led to the frigate's anchorage and the Russian village at S 40° W. The [westernmost] part of Unalaska Island was at S 62° W.[101]

THURSDAY, JULY 31 AT NOON TO FRIDAY, AUGUST 1. At noon, we remained anchored between the places mentioned above. At 5:30 P.M., we set full sail and headed southwest toward the bay. At nightfall, we realized the ebb tide was driving us away from the bay. At 9:30, we sent the launch ahead

[100] The present Unalaska Inlet.

[101] The present Cape Cheerful.

to sound with a lighted lantern. We were directly opposite the bay's entrance.

It dawned heavy with fog. We were almost inside the bay's entrance. The frigate was anchored there. At 8:30 A.M., the wind freshened through the entrance from the ESE and SE. It enabled us to tack the ship into the bay by 12:00 noon.

FRIDAY, AUGUST 1 AT MIDDAY TO SATURDAY, AUGUST 2. At 5:30 P.M., we tacked numerous times, hour by hour, without gaining headway inside the bay. As the wind became too strong, we went along side the bay's eastern shore as much as we could behind a point, which has a headland that looks like a monk. We anchored about two leagues from shore in fine black sand. The commander's ship was about one league away at the bottom of the bay. The Russian left immediately in his canoe with the two Indians. From this anchorage, the headland to the east of the bay was to the NE 05° E. Along with the [western] point, it formed the bay to the S 80° W. The northern part of the island that was outside and the island of Unalaska formed a canal to the N 30° E.

At dawn, there was a thick fog and a strong wind blew from the SE ¼ E. So we let out 200 fathoms of anchor line until there was two-thirds of the splice remaining. We passed the night with extreme watchfulness and care, because the wind howled and remained brisk. At dawn, it continued unabated.

SATURDAY, AUGUST 2 AT NOON TO SUNDAY, AUGUST 3. At noon, we remained anchored at the same location with a brisk wind blowing from the east-southeast. At 5:00 P.M., expecting another bad night, we hauled in as much of the anchor line as we could. We dropped anchor immediately off the port bow and then let out both anchor lines at the same time. The port one remained with 100 fathoms run out. The starboard one went out the same amount as it had the night before.

At nightfall, the wind blew hard and heavy clouds covered the sky and the land. But during the night, it began to calm down. By dawn it was almost calm, with a light wind blowing from the west-southwest. So we immediately began hauling in the port anchor. At 7:30, we began to veer toward the starboard anchor. At 9:00, it was hoisted. As it was almost calm, we started towing with the launch and, watching the sea gulls and foresails, we headed for the commander's anchorage. At 9:45, the wind blew from the southeast and we immediately took in all sail. We let the anchor fall in 40 fathoms of sand about four leagues away from the frigate.

SUNDAY, AUGUST 3 TO MONDAY, AUGUST 4. At midday, we remained anchored. At 5:00 P.M., the launch left for the frigate with an official report to the commander. At 10:00, it returned and we passed the night without incident.

At dawn, the frigate's launch arrived to give us a tow. At 10:15, we were close to the commander, so we dropped both the port and starboard anchors. At 1:00 P.M., the frigate's launch arrived with the commander and Captain Cusmiche,[102] the governor of this village. At 4:00 P.M., they returned to the frigate.[103] From this anchorage, the point to the east of the bay was to the northeast. The one further [west] was to the west-northwest. The Russian establishment was to the south, about three leagues away.

TUESDAY, AUGUST 5. At dawn, three men sick with scurvy were sent ashore in the commander's launch and our

[102]Potap Kuzmich Zaikof, the trader who wintered on Montague Island in 1783-84. Martínez had arrived at Unalaska Inlet July 21. Since then, the two men had shared numerous "banquets" and plenty of liquor. López de Haro was disgusted at finding Martínez living and carousing on shore with Zaikov.

[103]Narváez does not mention that Martínez, as soon as he came aboard the *San Carlos*, reviled López de Haro for the allegedly useless information he collected from Delarov as he had been able to learn all of it from Zaikov. In his report to the Viceroy on December 5, 1788, López de Haro described Martínez' departure as follows: "The least of his insults was to say all naval pilots were a bunch of rascally cabin boys, and that if he were on land he would give them thirty whacks; and leaving the cabin he went back aboard his own vessel declaring, in the presence of the seamen, that they were lousy. In view of such a scene, even the sailors were astonished, and those of us who were in the cabin would have been more surprised if we had not noted that all that happened was the effect of the excess of liquor he had in his body, as actually had been observed on different occasions, particularly in all the time he was in Prince William Sound. (See López de Haro's report to Flórez, December 5, 1788.)

launch went to a nearby river. During the day we collected 13 casks of water.[104]

WEDNESDAY, AUGUST 6. At 12:30, it stopped raining. The captain went in the launch to meet with Captain Cusmiche. So it was impossible to fill more than a few barrels of water. At 7:00 P.M., the launch returned with the captain. Nothing else of consequence happened.

THURSDAY, AUGUST 7. During the day, we filled six casks of water. It was noticed that the helm we had noted had given a heavy blow to the stern-post. Nothing else unusual happened, except for settling a big dispute.[105]

DESCRIPTION OF THE COAST BETWEEN CAPE GRENVILLE[106] AND UNALASKA ISLAND. *Cape Grenville's high mountains rise nearly perpendicular to the sea and the soundings meet the sea in no other way. Sailing WSW along the coast of this island*[107] *one will see the first islands to the northeast of Unalaska Island. These islands are moderately high and they form wide-mouthed canals. To the [west], they seem to offer good access to the sea. About one league away from them you will find 40 to 45 fathoms of water with a bottom of either rocks or black sand, coarse gravel and small shells.*

Continuing to sail along the shore of these islands about 152 leagues, you will see Unalaska Island to the SSW. This island is

[104]Again, Narváez judiciously omits an extraordinary incident. According to López de Haro's later report to the Viceroy, Martínez had summoned him to the *Princessa* that day with all his logs. He then placed the *San Carlos* under Narváez' command until López de Haro's "case" was decided. Pilot Juan Zayas and pilot's apprentice Antonio Palacios begged Martínez "on their knees" not to send the order. Enraged, Martínez threatened to remove the men from the packetboat and sink her. Martínez finally heeded the pilots' pleas, but he said that even if they all filed protests, he would beat them. (See Ibid.) On this same day, Martínez, some of his officers, a chaplain, and several crewmen gathered unobtrusively on shore and held a brief ceremony of possession, despite the fact that grounds for Russia's claims to sovereignty on the Alaskan coast by right of discovery had been laid by 1782.

[105]Narváez wrote *fuego grande en las entrar*, which makes no sense in this context unless it is taken as an idiomatic reference to the dispute between Martínez and López de Haro that saw the captain temporarily arrested and Narváez put in temporary command of the *San Carlos*. (See previous fn.)

[106]Cape Chiniak.

[107]It was actually the Alaskan Peninsula.

also steep. Near its northeast point there is a little mountain that looks like a sugar-loaf. To the NNW of this point, there is a small island[108] *that forms a narrow canal between it and the larger island. But the main canal*[109] *for going to the bay where the Russians have their establishment, or where they pass to the sheltered sea, is between this small island and the most southerly one in the chain [of islands] that are northeast of Unalaska Island.*

To enter inside the canal, one should wait for the current to turn to the [west]. If you are situated in the canal's mouth, it is possible to use a main topsail, even if the wind is to the prow. In this way it is possible to pass through the canal without trouble because it is easily passable.

When we were there, the current followed this pattern. At 8:00 A.M. it began flowing to the [west] with a little force, rising gradually because of the narrowness of the canal. At 12:00 noon, the current moved at about six nautical miles. From this hour, it gradually lost force until it stopped at nightfall. During the night it maintained the same force to the east.

If the wind is right, you will see a bay to the southwest in the eastern part of the canal. At the eastern point of the bay is a headland that looks like a friar. To reach it, remember that at this location the current does not flow directly [west], but moves somewhat to the NNW. If the wind blows outside 01° to 02° on the quintant, it will come through the middle of the canal and increase the current by a half-league. Two islands are close to Unalaska Island. These run north-south with two rocks that are also close to the coast of the island that forms the canal with Unalaska Island. These rocks are like sentinels over the water. They can be seen from the outside. From this spot, one can pass through the widest part of the canal. At a distance, one should start to direct oneself toward the bay on Unalaska Island as much as possible, so that a rising wind will allow you to enter far enough inside to drop anchor well within the point in 52 fathoms with a bottom of black sand. Be careful

[108]The present Unalga Island.

[109]Akutan Pass.

to drop the anchor close to land, because the bottom cannot be found three-quarters of a league from shore.

If the wind does not permit you to sail into the bay, it is possible to avoid being thrown about by the current by dropping anchor in 40 fathoms of water and good bottom next to the island that is north of Unalaska Island.

If there is enough wind to sail all the way into the bay's interior, it is advisable to enter by following the eastern coast and heading between two mountains that form a mouth that is much narrower than the bay's mouth. In the middle of these two mountains, you would drop the anchor in 25 fathoms and a good bottom. That location is about three or four leagues away from the Russian establishment, which lies at the south end of the bay.

FRIDAY, AUGUST 8. During the day, we towed the ship with three launches to reach the coast, which was about seven leagues away. There we found 40 to 45 fathoms of water with a bottom of dark sand and some shells.

[Description of Cape Grenville coast continued.] *The eastern part of this cape makes a cliff on the shore. In the middle of the course between this cliff and two points is an island that is very close to the cape's shore. To investigate all six islands, it is necessary to follow the eastern shore near the mountains. In this location, the most distinctive feature is an island with many large bays. Near the land is another small island to the [west]. That is the one which is close to the point on the [west] side of the bay, where the Russians have their establishment.*

Both of the points are high, but on the edges of the beach are a lot of banks, which are covered with green grass. It forms a cliff that looks like an island with two unusually large points. One faces [west] and the other east. The former is the one that forms the bay. This cape is two leagues long. The water is 20-25 fathoms deep, with a good bottom of coarse gravel. The course between these two points forms a large bay. In its interior, at the north end is where the Russians have their establishment.

This bay is very navigable. To go inside, it is necessary to stay away from the [west] point's shore, because two rocks thrust out to the [west] and always remain exposed. The bay has a bottom that is about six leagues long from north to south. Rounding the [western] point as you go from outside to the inside of the bay where the Russians have their establishment, you meet a cove that runs to the east. It makes the course look like an island that has two points. In this bay there is a large village of Indians. Continuing inside, one sees another cove farther north, in which there is a smaller village of Indians.

Inside the bay on the eastern coast, one finds various little houses made of cane that are Russian watchtowers. From the middle of the bay one can see a large house, which is a big storehouse. It is in the same village. The house cannot be seen nor can any landings be seen until a small point is rounded in the bay's interior. This little point and the shore form a small harbor that is very sheltered and plenty deep.

No wood can be found in the entire bay. It is impossible to enter the interior conveniently by water.

If [the weather] is reasonably clear, from the cape of two points, some islands can be seen to the southwest, including Trinidad Island[110]*, which is the biggest of the three.*

The Cape of Trinidad is nearly treeless and full of green grass. Close to it is a small, treeless island[111] *that is one of the three that make up Trinidad. To the south is the large island*[112] *where the Russians have a watchtower. There are 20–30 Indians living between this island and the coast. The water is 33 fathoms deep, but it is more shallow if one follows the coast to the east where there is a bay. In this bay, there are vast changes in the tides every six or seven hours.*

Rodiac Island,[113] *which runs ESE to WNW, is probably five*

[110]Unalaska Island.

[111]Unalga Island, to the north.

[112]Sedanka Island.

[113]The present Sanak Islands.

leagues long. It is a little high. Right next to it are many treeless islets full of green grass. About two or three leagues from this island is a good anchorage in 38 to 40 fathoms of water. Here it is possible to harbor ships and the fishing is excellent.

San Gonzalo Island[114] *is southwest of Punta Rotk*[115] *It is the largest of all the islands in that group and easily recognized by two mountains toward the middle of the island. The one to the south is a volcano.*[116] *This one has a very sharp point at the top. The one farther north is less high and ends in a less sharp point.*[117]

We made good speed towing the ship and collected several barrels of water.

SATURDAY, AUGUST 9. When we finished hauling the fresh water aboard, the crewmen were taken ashore to wash their clothes and cut grass. In the afternoon, we sent word to the commander that we were ready to sail whenever he was ready.

SUNDAY, AUGUST 10. After Mass, part of the crew and those in litters were sent ashore so they could pass some time and cut grass. At nightfall, they returned to the ship.

MONDAY, AUGUST 11. It rained all day, so no men were sent ashore. At night, the wind picked up again with strong gusts from the east-southeast.

TUESDAY, AUGUST 12. At 11:00 A.M., the captain went to the commander's ship in the launch. The commander ordered him, in case we got separated at sea, to follow the most direct route to the Port of Monterey [California]. At 2:00 P.M., the launch arrived with the captain. Because the weather was bad, it was impossible to send any men ashore. In the afternoon, we sent for our sick men.

WEDNESDAY, AUGUST 13. At 5:00 P.M., the frigate's launch arrived with the commander, who repeated to us his

[114]The present Unimak Island.

[115]The "Rocks of Cook" or the present Cape Pankof.

[116]Shishaldin Volcano, elevation 9372 ft.

[117]Pavlof Volcano, elevation 8905 ft.

order to head for Monterey, if the two ships got separated.[118] At 9:00 P.M., he left for his ship with two officers who had spent the afternoon on our ship.

THURSDAY, AUGUST 14. Some men were sent ashore for relaxation. Nothing else unusual happened.

FRIDAY, AUGUST 15. At 1:00 P.M., the commander's launch arrived carrying his officers, Captain Cusmiche and another Russian captain from a schooner that was anchored outside in one of the island's bays.[119] This captain had left his anchorage explicitly to see our ships.

SATURDAY, AUGUST 16. At dawn, it was calm. Nothing unusual happened.

SUNDAY, AUGUST 17. It rained a lot all day and the wind blew so hard we had to let out our long anchor line.[120] At 3:00 P.M., it began to calm.

Information Obtained at Unalaska Island

When we arrived at Unalaska Bay, we found the lone chief named Captain Cusmiche.[121] In his establishment there were two warehouses that were used to store otter pelts, whale sperm and various [equipment] used by the Russian fishery. In the entire establishment, there was only one house with a small room, in which Cusmiche lived.[122] Nearby there were about 20 huts, [occu-

[118]In his report to the Viceroy on December 5, 1788, López de Haro wrote that, during the ten days that both ships anchored at Unalaska Inlet, Martínez often hinted that "upon arriving at Monterey he intended requesting everyone's logs, and if he found any account of the trouble that had occurred, he would destroy it, and if he encountered in mine the slightest hint, he would take the packetboat away, arrest me and carry me to San Blas, and would deal rigorously with anyone found writing to [the Viceroy]."

This gave López de Haro and the other pilots a strong motive for reaching either Monterey or even San Blas ahead of Martínez, if they hoped to file a protest without his interference.

[119]Gavriil Pribylov, a member of the Corps of Naval Navigators working for the Aleutian commercial company of Lebedev-Lastochkin, had arrived from the Pribylov Islands in the Bering Sea aboard the schooner *Sv. Georgii.*

[120]111¼ fathoms long.

[121]Discovering that Zaikov was the only Russian at the outpost must have surprised the Spaniards, because Delarov had claimed 120 "Russians" were there. But it's possible that he was counting all those who worked for the Russians.

[122]Zaikov's quarters were attached to a large barracks.

pied by] Indians who hunted for the Russians.[123] *On the beach, we saw a schooner that had been hauled ashore on wooden rollers and shored up. Among the Indians on the island, one was unusually civilized. He was respected by the Russians for having been to [St.] Petersburg, where he had been honored by the Empress. The most powerful of all the Indians was the one who governed during the winter when Cusmiche was forced to retire to the other Russian outpost because of the unusually harsh, cold weather on this island and in its immediate surroundings.*

The establishment [at Unalaska Bay] was situated in very humid territory near the beach and at the edge of a river. There was no wood to be found on the entire island. The little that the Russians burned was that which the ocean left on the beach. When it became scarce, they [burned] a broom-like root for cooking.

The customs of these Indians were the same as those in Prince William Sound. They ate the same foods. The Russians treated them rigorously and required them to pay a tribute of three pesos per year to the Empress.

On the island we learned [the following information]. Some 60 Russians lived at Cape Rada[124] *and 120 lived at Unalaska Bay. The house that I saw at Prince William Sound was built by Captain Cusmiche the previous year.*[125] *All the Russians between the mainland and Unalaska Island totaled 500 men. They expected two frigates from Siberia to arrive in 1789. They are going to populate Prince William Sound immediately. Based on all this, we would say that the information we obtained at the establishment at [Three Saints Bay] was similar to that which we obtained on this island. The only differences were that here they denied that there was an establishment at Cape Elizabeth at 55°15' of latitude and 198°37' of longitude [west of] Greenwich and [they denied that] there was a canal that ran between the entrance to Cook's*

[123]All of them were Aleuts.

[124]Probably today's Afognak Island (See entry for July 1).

[125] See July 1 entry.

River and Cape Trinidad at 58°18' of latitude and 205°15' of longitude [west of] Greenwich.

To double check this information and find out if Captain Del Aro had deceived us at [Three Saints Bay], we asked where the remaining 320 Russians were located. They said these men were at Cape Rada and at the various lookouts. But this cannot be true, because we have seen that there was only a single Russian and some Indians at the watchtower on Cape Trinidad.[126] *The same thing happened at another watchtower to the north of Unalaska Island. We inferred that most of the men were at Cape Rada and that their true number was probably about the same as the number at Unalaska Bay and at [Three Saints Bay]. Nevertheless, we agreed that it was valuable for the packetboat to have visited both of the establishments at [Three Saints Bay] and Unalaska Bay or the Russians might have deceived us about their true numbers in these places.*

We did not doubt that there was a Russian establishment at Cook's River, because a [Russian] captain who had landed there wrote a letter to Captain Del Aro which was sent to [Three Saints Bay] along with an official message. Because he did not understand this letter, Captain Del Aro had brought it on board the packetboat and had asked us to see if it was written in Spanish or if there was someone on board who understood the language [in which it was written] so he could inform the Empress of its contents.[127] *When we saw it, we informed him that the letter was not written in either Spanish or French and that it appeared to be written in English. We informed Captain Del Aro that there was no one aboard who understood English. He let us copy it and told us that, because he could not decipher its contents, he would send it to the Empress.*

On the day that Captain Del Aro first examined the packetboat, we noticed that he was relaxed, spontaneous and appreciative of

[126]A point marked on López de Haro's chart to the north of *Islas Trinidad,* which is the present southern tip of the Aliulik Peninsula on Kodiak Island.

[127]See July 1 entry.

our friendly approach. He also laughed at the coincidence between his last name and that of our captain. Because of his friendly attitude, we have no doubts about the accuracy of the important information he gave us.

MONDAY, AUGUST 18 AT MIDDAY TO TUESDAY, AUGUST 19. At 8:30 A.M., the commander set sail and we followed at 9:00. In turn, we headed outside toward the N ¼ NE. At noon, we continued toward the N ¼ NE. The commander remained off our prow at a regular distance.

At 4:00 A.M., the thick fog cleared a bit and we saw that we were right next to the island that is north of Unalaska.[128] At 5:00, the commander was close to it, so he anchored and we headed for the same anchorage. At 8:00, we sounded several times near the frigate, without finding bottom. At 6:00, the same thing happened. At 6:30 A.M., we found bottom at 65 fathoms and dropped the port anchor. A very forceful current drove us toward the NNW, pushing us to leeward and carrying us away from the land. Dark storm clouds made it impossible to mark the land.

WEDNESDAY, AUGUST 20 AT NOON TO THURSDAY, AUGUST 21. At 9:00 A.M., the wind was strong and there were large swells. We had almost reached the end of the port anchor line that we had in the water. To splice more cable to it, we dropped the starboard anchor and drove from it while the splicing was done. At 11:00, we dropped the new anchor, and remained outside the port, riding on three cables. We could not see land well enough to mark it, because the strong wind whipped up the swollen sea and we were blanketed by rain and fog from the time we first anchored.

We passed the day with watchfulness and caution, hoping to remain at this anchorage until dawn, when we anticipated that it might clear. This morning we put the longboat inside because we feared losing it in the heavy seas.

[128]The present Akutan Island.

THURSDAY, AUGUST 21 AT NOON TO FRIDAY, AUGUST 22. At 2:00 P.M., during a break in the weather, we saw the commander setting sail toward the south.[129] It looked like he had hauled in his anchor lines. At 3:00, he came close to us but we noticed that he did not carry a launch, so we inferred that it had been lost. At this hour, he also tacked to the northwest and stowed his mainsail.

At dawn, it cleared up. I marked the southernmost part of the island that was north of Unalaska to the SSW and the northernmost part of another one that was further north to the E ¼ NE.[130] Between two other islands[131] there was another narrow canal that bore southeast and joined the larger pass[132] that we were in. We believed that there was a safe way through this canal. Because the [western] sea was almost calm and the wind was blowing almost noiselessly from the WSW, we decided to try sailing through it before the sea and the current drove us onto the southwest shore. With the prevailing wind, we were unable to leave through the pass by which we had entered, without ending up much farther north.

FRIDAY, AUGUST 22 AT NOON TO SATURDAY, AUGUST 23. At midday, the weather remained the same.

At dawn, there was a good wind to the [west]. So we set sail to see if, by tacking to windward, we could reach the south-southeastern point of the island and enter the pass through which we had come in. At 8:30 P.M., we raised the anchor and ran up the top mainsails. A little later, we ran up the mainsails, with the wind coming from the WSW. But the fog closed in and we could not see the land. At 12:00 noon, we tacked into a south wind toward the WSW.

SATURDAY, AUGUST 23 AT NOON TO SUNDAY, AUGUST 24. At 1:30 P.M., the fog cleared and we saw that we were farther

[129]Through Unimak Pass.

[130]The present Unimak Island.

[131]The present Akun Island and Akutan Island.

[132]Unimak Pass.

in the bay formed by the two islands. So we followed our course to come alongside the southern island. At 3:30, we realized that we could not get out by tacking to windward and the current was about to drive us onto the shore of the northernmost island, because it was becoming calm. We dropped the port anchor in 43 fathoms with a bottom of dark sand.

From there, under full sail, we bore toward the south shore of the island that is to the north, [which is] to the SW of the pass that we had sighted to the southeast. The northern part of the other island that forms the canal was to the ENE, about one league away.

At 9:00 A.M., two Indians and a Russian lookout arrived in a canoe. The Russian told us that there was no way to get through the canal to the southeast and that there was another pass farther north.[133] At 11:30, we raised the anchor and set sail toward this pass.

SUNDAY, AUGUST 24 AT MIDDAY TO MONDAY, AUGUST 25. At noon, the Russian left in his canoe. At 5:15 P.M., the wind remained calm, so we dropped the port anchor in 40 fathoms of water. Under full sail, we bore toward the [western] shore of an island [that was] to the WSW.

The point that was south of the canal's mouth was an island to the east. The one to the north was the southernmost part of San Gonzalo Island,[134] which was ENE 05° N. The land seen farther north of this island was to the NNE, about four leagues from the canal's mouth.

MONDAY, AUGUST 25 AT NOON TO TUESDAY, AUGUST 26. At noon, we continued toward the E ¼ NE under full sail. The night was ugly. At 9:00 P.M., the waves were hitting us hard from the stern toward the north. Fearing we would be driven into the Bay of Bristol[135] by these winds, we dropped anchor in 70 fathoms, carrying full sail. We passed the rest of

[133]Unimak Pass.

[134]The present Unimak Island.

[135]The large bay northeast of the Alaskan Peninsula.

the night this way until dawn. At 9:00, we raised the anchor, trimmed sail and headed again toward the E ¼ NE, searching for the canal.

TUESDAY, AUGUST 26 AT NOON TO WEDNESDAY, AUGUST 27. At noon, we tacked to the SSW under full sail, with the aim of finding a good anchorage where we could wait for the wind to veer 03° or 04° on the quintant. Otherwise, the current and the wind would drive us northward. At 1:00 P.M., we sounded in 45 fathoms, dropped anchor and took in all sail. From there, the fog made it impossible to make any markings.

At dawn, a fresh wind blew from NW to SE, so we swung around on the anchor line. At 8:00 A.M., we weighed anchor, raised the top mainsails and foresails, and headed into the wind in search of the canal. At 8:30, we continued under full sail.

Note: On leaving Unalaska Bay, the weak winds and stiff currents forced us to anchor off the [western] part of the island that is north of Unalaska. There we observed that the current ran north and north-northwest with much force. Winds from the southeast and south-southeast made it impossible to depart through the canal by which we had entered.[136] Each time we tried to leave, it proved impossible because the wind blew from the west and the west-southwest and the current neither let up nor stopped flowing north. The only way we could succeed was to wait for fresh winds from the north and the north-northwest.

From this location, one wants to seize the first opportunity to sail along the coast of Unalaska Island to the pass between San Gonzalo Island[137] and the island to the northeast of Unalaska.[138] This canal[139] is wide, but it must be without strong currents if one expects to depart this way. Even if the

[136] Akutan Pass.

[137] The present Unimak Island.

[138] The present Krenitizin Islands.

[139] The present Unimak Pass.

winds are favorable, they must be fresh enough to overcome the current.

Sailing along the shores of these islands through the canal, one sees several narrow channels formed by the islands. We were unable to investigate these channels because of the difficulties we experienced. All our information came from the Russian sentinel, who said the one we had sighted on entering the canal did not have a clear passage. So we inferred that the others were the same.

Following the coasts of these islands, one must be careful to approach them by anchoring in at least four fathoms of water. As the shores are all clean, it is possible to drop anchor quickly in calm weather. But it is necessary to be extremely careful, especially when the winds are rising and fresh, to avoid being carried north of the canal by the strong current that never lets up. If that happens, it would take a great deal of work to sail south, as imperative as this may be. So, if you are already north of San Gonzalo Island, it is essential to know that there is no other pass except the one near the point of San Gonzalo Island.[140] The Russians said the [only other] canal was no more than one fathom deep.[141]

This island [San Gonzalo] is extremely rugged. Throughout the time we were there, the weather was foul and the fog was heavy. Strong currents and unfavorable wind conditions made it almost impossible to navigate.

WEDNESDAY, AUGUST 27 AT NOON TO THURSDAY, AUGUST 28. At noon, we used the launch to tow the ship eastward. By 4:00, we were outside the canal. At 4:30, we brought the launch aboard. At 5:00, we headed toward the SE ¼ E, so we would be ready to sail away from the island under full sail. At 7:00, we marked the island that is to the north of San Gonzalo[142] and forms a canal[143] at N 72° W, about five

[140]Unimak Pass. [141]Probably the present False Pass, further northeast.

[142]Actually, the southern tip of the Alaskan Peninsula. [143]False Pass.

leagues away. At dawn, we saw the island that is south of San Gonzalo in the NW ¼ N and the island with which it forms the canal in the W ¼ NW, about seven or eight leagues away. At 6:00, we headed S ¼ SE. It was impossible to make an observation, so I used dead reckoning to estimate our point of departure at 54°15'N of latitude and 59°00' of longitude, which I believed was our point of departure.

THURSDAY, AUGUST 28 AT NOON TO FRIDAY, AUGUST 29. At 4:00 P.M., the fore-topsail ripped as we brought it in to examine it. We left it hanging over the yards for repairs. As it was impossible to fix, we trimmed the top-mainsail to a little more than half and the fore-topsail was unbent to bend the sails another [notch].

At 7:00 A.M., the fore-topsail was bent. It remained over the yards because it was calm. It was impossible to make an observation.

FRIDAY, AUGUST 29 TO NOON SATURDAY, AUGUST 30. At noon, we continued under full sail. From my observation, I found a difference of 33' longitude during the last three days, which I corrected.

SATURDAY, AUGUST 30 AT NOON TO SUNDAY, AUGUST 31. At sunrise, I took an observation at 18°43' of variation NE.

MONDAY, SEPTEMBER 8 AT MIDDAY TO TUESDAY, SEPTEMBER 9. At noon, we remained under full sail. At 12:00, the captain called all of us to a meeting.[144] He informed us of changes in our route that he had made since we had separated from the commander near Unalaska Island. He said the changes had prevented us from fulfilling our orders to follow the coast starting at 60°N[145] latitude, with the aim of charting and reconnoitering [to the south] all that was possible in the time that we had left, as the Viceroy had instructed. [The cap-

[144]Narváez called it a *junta.*

[145]It's unclear whether Narváez wrote 50 or 60 degrees, but the latter makes more sense, because López de Haro's chart notes that the entire coast between Juan de Fuca Strait in the north to 50° N "was seen but not charted."

tain said] he believed we were 100 leagues from the continent.[146] He argued that it would be inconvenient to follow the coastal route at this time of year. He thought it was wiser to head directly for San Blas, so that we would have a direction to run in if we encountered stiff headwinds. He also noted that, at Unalaska Island, the commander had ordered him, in case of separation, to take a route directly to the garrison [at San Blas].[147]

We told him we all agreed with his decision. There was not enough time to survey the land in this kind of bad weather, because constant fog and rain on most days permitted only a league of clearing.

WEDNESDAY, SEPTEMBER 10 AT MIDDAY TO THURSDAY, SEPTEMBER 11. At midday, we continued fully rigged. At 4:00 P.M., we steered the helm SSE, with the aim of staying well clear of the coast, because the weather was sufficiently ugly. The wind blew hard in strong gusts. The fog closed in and we experienced squalls and heavy rain.

SUNDAY, SEPTEMBER 28 AT MIDDAY TO MONDAY, SEPTEMBER 29. At midday we continued fully rigged. At 8:00 A.M., several penguins, dolphins, and birds passed.

TUESDAY, SEPTEMBER 30 AT MIDDAY TO WEDNESDAY, OCTOBER 1. At noon, we continued under full sail. We concentrated on looking for land, but nothing was seen.

WEDNESDAY, OCTOBER 1 AT NOON TO THURSDAY, OCTOBER 2. At noon, we continued under full sail, hoping to sight land during the day. At sunset, a good reconnaissance was made but nothing was seen. It dawned beautifully clear and serene. But we could not see land. So we again headed toward the E ¼ SE.

---

[146]They were off San Francisco, headed directly for Monterey.

[147]In asking the pilots to support his decision to disobey Martínez' orders to rendezvous at Monterey, López de Haro was exposing all the officers to charges of insubordination. But the López de Haro faction shared a common motivation: by returning directly to San Blas they could lodge their complaints before Martínez arrived and exercised his influence.

THURSDAY, OCTOBER 2 AT NOON TO FRIDAY, OCTOBER 3. At sunrise, a good reconnaissance was made but no land was seen. At dawn, we still could not see land. We searched the horizon all day without success. At 8:00 P.M., we saw several sticks, but nothing else of interest.

FRIDAY, OCTOBER 3 AT MIDDAY TO SATURDAY, OCTOBER 4. At sunrise, I made a good reconnaissance without sighting land. At dawn, not a single sign of land was seen.

SATURDAY, OCTOBER 4 AT NOON TO SUNDAY, OCTOBER 5. At 2:30 P.M., several sticks passed by. At sunrise, I made a very good reconnaissance from the mast head, but nothing was seen. No land was seen at dawn, but we raised full sail. At 7:00, we saw a leafy tree [float by], but nothing else of interest.

SUNDAY, OCTOBER 5 AT MIDDAY TO MONDAY, OCTOBER 6. At sunrise, a good reconnaissance was made from the mast head, but no land was sighted.

Note: At midday, we were still north of the island of high land. This morning, we saw several sticks, leafy trees and sea gulls pass by.

MONDAY, OCTOBER 6 AT NOON TO TUESDAY, OCTOBER 7. At sunrise, a good reconnaissance was made from the mast head and land was seen to the NNE at a great distance, but it was too far away to mark. At noon, the northwestern end of Guadalupe Island was marked by the compass running to the NNE. I estimated we were at 14°20' of longitude, which differed from the dead reckoning by 570 minutes, or 430 nautical miles in distance from the most easterly point.

TUESDAY, OCTOBER 7 AT NOON TO WEDNESDAY, OCTOBER 8. At sunset, I observed 05° of variation NE.

THURSDAY, OCTOBER 9 AT NOON TO FRIDAY, OCTOBER 10. At sunset, 05° of variation NE was observed again.

TUESDAY, OCTOBER 14 AT MIDDAY TO WEDNESDAY, OCTOBER 15. At sunset, 05° of variation NE was observed.

Nothing usual was seen. At 12:00 P.M., we held off mounting full sail, so that we would not cover the full distance that we believed remained before we reached the coast. At sunrise, a good reconnaissance was made and land was seen. So we raised full sail.

WEDNESDAY, OCTOBER 15 AT MIDDAY TO THURSDAY, OCTOBER 16. At sunrise, a good reconnaissance from the mast head was made, but the land was not seen. At dawn, it was sighted unclearly because of a sandstorm.

At sunrise, I marked San Blas at S 72° E, about eight to nine leagues away with the nearest coast five to six leagues distant. We tacked to the east. At 8:30 we tacked ESE.

Note: [On sighting land], I found the latitude differed by 93' to the east, or 68 nautical miles in distance.

THURSDAY, OCTOBER 16 AT MIDDAY TO FRIDAY, OCTOBER 17. At noon, we caught a glimpse of the land and marked it. At 6:00 P.M., Cape San Lucas was to the N 23° W and the northeasternmost part of the coast was to the N 25° E at a distance of three or four leagues from the former. At dawn, the land was in sight, but obscured by heavy fog. At sunrise, I observed 28° of variation NE. We arrived [at Cape San Lucas] at midday

SATURDAY, OCTOBER 18 AT MIDDAY TO SUNDAY, OCTOBER 19. At sunset, a good reconnaissance from the mast head was made, but the Marías Islands were not seen. At 6:00, we set a course to the E 05° N, with the aim of cutting between the islands until the moon came out, which it did at 10:00 P.M. As it was clear and beautiful, we headed SE 05° E. At dawn, we saw the Marías Islands and I marked them upon leaving the southeasternmost island. The northernmost island was at S 38° E and San Ignacio was at S 28° E, and we were about three leagues from the latter. Based on my point of demarcation, Isabela Island was E 03° S about 16½ leagues away and the port of San Blas was 33 leagues away to the E ¼ SE.

SUNDAY, OCTOBER 19 AT MIDDAY TO MONDAY, OCTOBER 20. At noon, I observed our latitude at 21°34'N and marked the southernmost part of the island southeast of the Marías Islands to the south. I estimated that we were at 01° west of San Blas. We were headed toward the White Rock,[148] which was 11 leagues away to the east and the port of San Blas was 17 leagues away.

At 6:00 P.M., the southernmost of the Marías Islands was to the S 10° E and the most northerly one—San Juanito Island—was at S 41° W, about three or four leagues away.

At sunrise, the most northerly of the Marías Islands (San Juanito Island) was to the W 04° S and the southernmost island was to the S 14° E, about two or three leagues from the former. We arrived [at the Marías Islands] at midday.

MONDAY, OCTOBER 20 AT MIDDAY TO TUESDAY, OCTOBER 21. At noon, we were at 21°24'N of latitude. The southernmost of the Marías Islands was to the W ¼ SE. I estimated the true longitude at 25 minutes west of San Blas. The coast was in the E ¼ NE, about 24 nautical miles away.

At 5:00 P.M., after noting that there had been two days when the sea was not pitching much to the south, we headed NE 05° N. At 6:00, the northernmost of the Marías Islands was marked on the compass to the northwest at N 80° W and the southernmost island was to the southeast in the SW ¼ S, about four leagues away.

At sunrise, the northernmost of the Marías Islands was to the northwest at W ¼ NW and the southernmost island was to the S 53° W, about five leagues away. At 11:00, the wind freshened in the north and we continued, springing the mast as much as possible. At this hour, the entire coast was visible to us.

TUESDAY, OCTOBER 21 AT MIDDAY TO WEDNESDAY, OCTOBER 22. At midday, we continued under full sail with

[148] A landmark by which the port of San Blas was recognized.

the wind to the NE 05° N. At 2:15, we saw the White Rock to the NNE from the outside. At 1:00, we launched our ship's boats. At 5:00, the wind shifted to the SSW and it calmed down.

At sundown, the White Rock was to the N 05° E and the high land of San Juan[149] was to the E ¼ SE, about two leagues away from the former. At 7:00 P.M., it was calm, so we hauled in all sails and dropped the starboard anchor in 27 fathoms, muddy bottom.

At noon, we saw the village of San Blas to the ENE, about three leagues away.

WEDNESDAY, OCTOBER 22 AT NOON TO THURSDAY, OCTOBER 23. At midday, we headed to the ENE 05° N toward the port under full sail. The wind was not quite fresh. At 3:00, we hauled in the top-gallant, studding sails and stay sails. At 3:15, we were close to the inside of the White Rock, so we clewed up the major sails. A little later, we lowered the boats, dropped anchor in five fathoms—loose mud bottom—and furled all the rigging.

The village of San Blas was to the NE ¼ E, the beach was to the north and the White Rock was outside to the W ¼ NW.

Note: On reaching land in the entrance of Prince Carlos, I checked Cook's chart, because it did not match the Spanish chart [of 1799]. I set out to convert the longitude based on the Greenwich meridian to the one of San Blas, taking into account that we placed San Blas at 254°30' west of Greenwich. I found a great difference between this meridian and the one of Paris. At present the Port of San Blas is falsely considered to be 254°30' west of Paris, when it is actually 255°15' west of Greenwich. The points of demarcation will be corrected on the chart of this expedition so that the longitude of Greenwich will agree with the one of Paris. The difference has been ascertained from the astronomical observation placing

[149]The *Serro del San Juan* was high ground east of San Blas.

the Cape of San Lucas at 102°20'[150] west of the Paris meridian,[151] from which longitude this expedition's chart is plotted.

JOSÉ MARÍA NARVÁEZ[152]

GLOSSARY OF PLACES MENTIONED IN JOURNAL

SPANISH	TRANSLATION	TODAY
3-8-1788		
Puerto de San Blas	Port of San Blas	San Blas
3-9		
Islas de las Marías	Islas Marías	Islas Marías
5-16		
Isla Montaguo	Montague Island	Montague Island
Entrada del Principe Guillermo	Prince William Sound	Prince William Sound
Entrada del Principe Carlos	Prince Carlos Sound	Valdez Arm
5-17		
....	....	Hinchinbrook Entrance
5-19		
Islitas Navzas	Little Navzas Islands	Middleton Island
Islas de Hijosa	Hijosa Islands	Middleton Island
5-21		
Ribera de Cook	Cook's River	Cook's Inlet
6-1		
Puerto de Flórez on the northwest side of Montague Island	Port of Flórez	An unidentified bay

[150] Narváez may have written 107°20'.

[151] Previously, the Spaniards considered San Blas to be 107°06' west of Paris, which was not quite correct, because it was based on an estimated difference of five degrees between San Blas and Cape San Lucas, which is not that much further west.

[152] The manuscript was signed by Narváez.

6-7		
Trinidas	Trinidad	Alaskan Peninsula Trinity Islands Unalaska
6-10		
Islas Vertis	Green Islands	Green Island
Puerto de Santiago	Port Santiago	Port Etches
6-11		
....	....	Montague Peak
6-16		
Isla San Antonio	San Antonio Island	La Touche and Elrington Islands
6-23		
Volcan de Miranda	Miranda Volcano	Iliamna Volcano
Cabo Elizavel	Cape Elizabeth	Portlock at SE tip of Kenai Peninsula
6-26		
Cabo Grenvellia		
Cabo Grenville	Cape Grenville	Cape Chiniak
6-27		
Cabo dos Puntos	Cape of Two Points	Sitkalidak Island
6-28		
....	....	Sitkalidak Strait
6-29		
....	....	Twoheaded Island
6-30		
....	Three Saints Bay	
....		Shelikof Strait
7-1		
Islas de Trinidad	Trinity Islands	Trinity Islands
Cabo Rada	Cape Rada	Afognak Island
7-3		
....	....	Sitkinak Island
7-6		
Isla Foggi	Foggy Island	Chirikof Island
(Isla Infante)	....	Chirikof Island
7-9		
(Islas de los Pilotos)	....	Shumagin Islands
Isla Onalaska	Unalaska Island	Unalaska Island

7-11		
Isla Rodiac	Rodiac Island	Sanak Islands
(Zayas ó Plíes)	....	Sanak Islands
7-13,16;8-8		
Cabo Alvides	Cape Alvides	Cape Pankof?
Cabo Rook	Rocks of Cook	Cape Pankof
Punta Rotk	Rocks of Cook	Cape Pankof
7-16		
San Gonzalo	San Gonzalo	Unimak Island
(Mt. Fernandez)	....	Shishaldin Volcano
7-17		
....	....	Tigalda Island
7-18		
Cape Providencia	Cape Providence	Cape Biorka?
....	....	Akutan Pass
....	....	Akutan Island
7-19		
....	....	Krenitzin Islands
7-29		
Onalaska	Unalaska	Unalaska
....	....	Unalaska Bay
7-31		
....	....	Unalaska Inlet
8-8		
....	....	Unalga Island
Islas Trinidad	Trinidad Island	Unalaska Island
....	....	Sedanka Island
....	....	Pavlof Volcano
8-17		
Cabo Trinidad	Cape Trinidad	South tip of Aliulik Peninsula on Kodiak Island
8-21, 28		
....	....	Unimak Pass
8-25		
Bahia de Bristol	Bay of Bristol	Bristol Bay
8-27		
....	....	Krenitzin Islands
....	....	False Pass

10-6		
Isla Guadalupe	Guadalupe Island	Guadalupe Island
10-16		
Cabo San Lucas	Cape San Lucas	Cape San Lucas
10-19		
Isla San Ignacio	San Ignacio Island	San Ignacio Island
Isla San Isavela	San Isabela Island	San Isabela Island
La Piedra Blanca	White Rock	White Rock
Isla San Juanico	San Juanito Island	San Juanito Island
10-21		
Serro del San Juan	high land of San Juan	high ground east of San Blas

Appendices

APPENDIX A

A Schooner's Three Lives (1788-1792)

The complex origins of the *Santa Saturnina* have been examined in greatest detail by Warren Cook in *Flood Tide of Empire.* But a few of the key sources that he cites leave some room for different interpretations. The following appears to be the most probable chronology. (Refer to text for entries without sources.)

DATE	EVENT
March 30, 1788	Chinese carpenters aboard English merchant captain John Meares' ship prepare "moulds and model for a sloop of fifty tons that was designed to be built immediately on our arrival in (Nootka Sound)."[1]
June 5, 1788	Meares has had keel laid for construction of a "vessel of 40 or 50 tons" at Friendly Cove.[2]
Sept. 20, 1788	*Northwest America* launched at Friendly Cove by Meares.[3]
Sept. 24, 1788	Meares leaves English fur trader Robert Funter in command of *Northwest America* at Friendly Cove and instructs him to winter in Sandwich (Hawaiian) Islands and rendezvous at Friendly Cove in the spring.[4]
October 27, 1788	Funter sails for Hawaii in command of *Northwest America.*[5]
April 19, 1789	Funter returns to Friendly Cove in command of *Northwest America,* sails northward one week later in search of pelts, and returns June 8.[6]
June 9, 1789	*Northwest America* seized from Funter at Friendly Cove by Spanish captain Estevan José Martínez.[7]
June 19/20, 1789	Confiscated *Northwest America* reconditioned at Friendly Cove and rechristened *Santa Gertrudis la Magna* by Father Severo Patero.[8]

---

[1] Meares, John, *Voyages Made in the Years 1788 and 1789...*, p. 88.

[2]Ibid., p. 116.

[3]Ibid., p. 220-22.

[4]Ibid., p. 222-25.

[5]Ibid., p. 334.

[6]Cook, Warren, *Flood Tide of Empire,* p. 146-47, 160.

[7]Ibid., p. 160.

[8]Martínez, Esteban José, *Diario de la Navagacion...*, p. 78-79. British mariners, who had come from Asia, considered the date to be June 20.

June 21, 1789	Martínez sends José Narváez in the *Santa Gertrudis la Magna* to investigate already discovered Clayoquot Sound, Barkley Sound, and Juan de Fuca Strait.[9]
July 5, 1789	Narváez returns to Friendly Cove on the *Santa Gertrudis la Magna.*
July 29 to Aug. 1	Martínez starts using unfinished pieces of a new schooner under construction near Friendly Cove and unassembled parts of the *Jason* (seized aboard the *Argonaut* from the English captain James Colnett on July 2-3) to make *Santa Gertrudis la Magna* more seaworthy.[10]
October 20, 1789	Alterations of *Santa Gertrudis la Magna* completed: planks replaced, ribs added, gunnels raised, and lengthened a yard.[11]
October 30, 1789	Martínez places José Verdía in command of *Santa Gertrudis la Magna* and it leaves Friendly Cove for San Blas.[12]
December 6, 1789	*Santa Gertrudis la Magna* arrives in San Blas.[13]
February 3, 1790	Bodega y Quadra has *Santa Gertrudis la Magna* dismantled at San Blas and returned in pieces to Friendly Cove by Francisco Eliza, new commandant at Nootka.[14]
May 1790	Captain Pedro Alberni supervises laying of keel for new schooner at Friendly Cove.[15]
September 1790	New schooner launched at Friendly Cove.[16]
November 1, 1790	New schooner christened *Santa Saturnina,* alias *Orcasitas,* at Friendly Cove.[17]
Winter 1790-91	*Santa Saturnina, Concepción,* and *Princesa* ride out winter months unrigged at Friendly Cove.[18]
January 4, 1791	Captain Colnett finds *Santa Saturnina, Concepción,* and *San Carlos* (actually *Princesa*) riding at anchor in Friendly Cove.[19]
March 1, 1791	Colnett nearly recovers *Santa Saturnina* from Eliza.[20]
April 3, 1791	Eliza orders Narváez to use *Santa Saturnina* to scout entrance to Nootka Sound for five English or Russian ships.[21]

---

[9]Ibid., p. 79.

[10]Ibid., p. 100-101. Also see: Colnett, *The Journals. . .*, 204, n204; Cook, op. cit., 188-9, n188; Wagner, *Spanish Explorations. . .*, 137, 141; Howay, *Voyages of the Columbia,* 227n.

[11]Martínez, op. cit., p. 131; Cook, op. cit., 192.

[12]Ibid., p. 132; 193.

[13]Cook, op. cit., p. 194.

[14] Ibid., p. 276, 276n; Wagner, op. cit., 141.

[15] Cook, op. cit., p. 276.

[16]Kendrick, John, *The Men with Wooden Feet,* p. 45.

[17]Cook, op. cit., p. 276, 276n; Wagner, op. cit., p. 141; Howay, op. cit., n227.

[18]Cook, op. cit., p. 294.

[19]Colnett, op. cit., p. 204.

[20]Ibid., p. 206-7.

[21]Cook, op. cit., p. 297.

May 4, 1791	Major expedition, with Eliza in command of the *San Carlos* and Narváez in command of the *Santa Saturnina,* leaves Friendly Cove to explore inside Juan de Fuca Strait.[22]
June 11, 1791	Both ships rendezvous at Cordova (Esquimalt).
June 14-24, 1791	Juan Pantoja commands *Santa Saturnina* to explore southern Gulf Islands in Juan de Fuca Strait.
June 28, 1791	*Santa Saturnina* and *San Carlos* anchor at Puerto de Quadra (Port Discovery) on south side of Juan de Fuca Strait.
July 1-22, 1791	Narváez commands *Santa Saturnina* to explore Georgia Strait.
July 26, 1791	*Santa Saturnina,* with pilot Juan Carrasco in command, and *San Carlos* leave Puerto de Quadra and head north for Nootka Sound.
August 14, 1791	*Santa Saturnina* and *San Carlos* get separated.
August 28, 1791	Headwinds force Carrasco to sail *Santa Saturnina* south to Monterey.
Sept. 15, 1791	Carrasco arrives at Monterey on *Santa Saturnina.*
October 16, 1791	Carrasco leaves Monterey on *Santa Saturnina* and heads for San Blas.
November 9, 1791	Carrasco arrives at San Blas on *Santa Saturnina* and delivers results of Narváez' explorations to Bodega, prompting another expedition.
June 1792	Carrasco sent from San Blas to Friendly Cove in command of *Santa Saturnina* with urgent instructions advising Bodega to hang on to Nootka as long as possible.[23]
Sept. 1792	Carrasco reaches San Francisco on *Santa Saturnina.*[24]
October 21, 1792	Bodega sends López de Haro from San Francisco to Friendly Cove on *Santa Saturnina* with instructions for Fidalgo.[25]
Dec. 23, 1792	*Santa Saturnina* returns to San Francisco.[26]

[22]Wagner, op. cit., p. 142.
[23]Cook, op. cit., p. 386-87.
[24]Ibid., p. 387.
[25]Ibid.
[26]Ibid.

APPENDIX B

Dimensions of the *Santa Saturnina*

I have found two sets of information about the *Santa Saturnina's* dimensions. These use different units of measure for length and beam, but they appear equivalent. Wagner, quoting both Eliza and Pantoja, refers to *codos* ("elbows").[1] The manifest for the *Santa Saturnina,* located in the Museo Naval, Madrid,[2] uses *pies* (feet) and *pulgadas* (inches).

MEASUREMENTS	WAGNER	MANIFEST
Length on keel	18.0 *codos*	36.0 *pies*
Beam	6.5 *codos*	13.0 *pies*
Draft aft	5.5 *pies*	5.0 *pies* 6 *pulgadas*
Draft at bow	4.0 *pies*	4.0 *pies*

The precise length of a *codo*—a crude elbow to finger-tip measurement that was only used by shipbuilders—is uncertain. According to Wagner, it was either 33/48 of a standard *vara* (yard) or 27.5/40 of the shipbuilder's *vara.* According to the *Dictionario Maritimo Espanol,* these equivalents (.6875 of a *vara*) are equal to 24.75 *pulgadas* (inches).

According to Kenyon,[3] the *pulgada* was 0.912 of an English inch. That would make a *pie* (12 *pulgadas* or 12 x 0.912) equal to 10.944 English inches. Thus, a *codo* was equal to 21.888 English inches or about 1-foot-10-inches and a *vara* was 32.832 English inches or about 2-feet-9-inches.

TABLE OF EQUIVALENCES

		of a vara		pulgadas	inches	feet	ft. & in.
vara	40/40	48/48	1.0000	36.000	32.832	2.736	2'9"
codo	27.5/40	33/48	0.6875	24.000	21.888	1.824	1'10"
pie	12.5/40	15/48	0.3125	12.000	10.944	.912	11"
pulgada	1.04/40	1.25/48	0.0260	1.000	.912		

[1]Wagner, Henry R., *Spanish Explorations...,* pp. 141, n141, 182

[2]See Appendix C.

[3]Kenyon, Malcolm Hall, "Naval Construction and Repair in San Blas."

Applying these figures first to Wagner's Spanish dimensions and then to those of the manifest, the English equivalents would be the same in both instances:

WAGNER'S DIMENSIONS:

Length on keel	18.0 codos	x 21.888 in.=	393.984 in.	=32.83 ft.=32'10"
Beam	6.5 codos	x 21.888 in.=	142.272 in.	=11.86 ft. =11'10"
Draft aft	5.5 pies	x 10.944 in.=	60.192 in.	= 5.02 ft. = 5'
Draft at bow	4.0 pies	x 10.944 in.=	43.776 in.	= 3.65 ft. = 3'8"

MANIFEST'S DIMENSIONS:

Length on keel	36.0 pies	x 10.944 in.=	393.984 in.	=32.83 ft. =32'10"
Beam	13.0 pies	x 10.944 in. =	142.272 in.	=11.86 ft. =11'10"
Draft aft	5.0 pies	x 10.944 in.=	54.720 in.	
	6.0 pul.	x .912 in.=	5 .472 in.	
			60 .192 in.	= 5.02 ft. = 5'
Draft at bow	4.0 pies	x 10.944 in.=	43 .776 in.	= 3.65 ft. = 3'8"

Appendix C

Manifest of the *Santa Saturnina*

MANIFEST[1] showing the state of the 4-cannon schooner *Santa Saturnina,* alias *Horcasitas,* commanded by Second Pilot of the Royal Fleet Don José Narváez, when he sailed from this Port of the Holy Cross of Nootka.

Officers	Infantry	Petty Officers	Gunners	Seamen	Boys	Servants	Total
2	5	2	5	5	2	1	22

Anchors	Cables	Rank & Number of Officers	Sails	
1: 6 *quin.*	1: 5 *pul.*	Captain & Second Pilot:	Mainsails	2
	2: 3 *pul.*	Don José Narváez	Foresails	2
Small Anchors:		Pilotin & Second Officer:	Square Sail	2
1 iron: 2 *aroba*		Don Juan Carrasco	Staysails	2
1 iron: 3 *aroba*			Jib	1

Dimensions & Stores of Vessel	*pies.*	*pul.*
Keel (oakum to oakum)	36	
Beam	13	
Length (perp. to perp.)	39	
Depth of hold	5	6
Plan (width of hold)	5	
Draft - aft	5	6
Draft - foreward	4**	
Drag	1	6
Ballast	60	*quin.*
Burden	32	*tonales*

Guns, Munitions, Firearms	
Cannons, bronze 3 lb.	2*
Swivel Guns	3
Roundshot 3 lb.	100
Bags of Grapeshot	130
Roundshot 2 lb.	200
Muskets	9
Bayonets	9
Pistols	12
Swords	4

[1]Translated from original Spanish document by Museo Naval,

Flintlock		Victuals & Water	
Pikes	5	Rations at the standard rate:	
Musket balls of lead	1 aroba	800 units for 40 days per 20 persons	
Gunflints	42		
Powder	116 lbs.		
Cartridges for Cannon	69	Barrels of Water	24

Attestation — This vessel sailed seaworthy, with masts, spars and standing and running rigging in good order and with the standard spare spars.

Notes: 1. *Quin.: Quintal* = 112 English lbs.
2. *Pul.*: *Pulgada* (Spanish inch) = 0.912 of English inch
3. Small anchors: grapnels with 4 flukes
4. *Aroba* = 1/4 *quintal* or 28 lbs.
5. *Pie de Burgo* = 0.912 English feet
6. Perp. to perp.: between perpendiculars
7. *Tonal: tonelada* or Spanish ton
* According to Eliza: 4
** According to Pantoja: 4 1/2

Appendix D

Descendants of Antonio Narváez

1 Antonio Narváez
+Ursula Gervete
2 José María Narváez b. 1768 in Cádiz, Spain; d. 04-08-1840 in Guadalajara, Mexico
+María Leonarda Aleja Maldonado m. 23-10-1796 in Tepic
3 José Narváez b. 1797 d. 01-09-1802
3 José María Miguel Narváez b. 30-09-1798
3 Francisco de Paula Guadalupe de Jesus Narváez b. 03-04-1801 in Tepic; d. 23-05-1884 in Tepic
+Josefa Labastida y Bravo b. 03-11-1815 in Tepic; m. 23-06-1835 in Tepic; d. 15-11-1887 in Tepic
4 José Francisco Julio Ataulfo Narváez b. 13-04-1836
4 Rosa Blanco Leonarda Abraham Narváez b. 16-03-1837
4 María Margarita Sixta de Refugio Narváez b. 26-03-1838 in Tepic; d. 23-05-1884 in Tepic
+Edward Weber b. 1831 in Germany; m. 24-04-1859 in Tepic; d. 23-05-1884 in Tepic
5 Margarita Weber b. 19-01-1860 in Tepic
+José López Portillo y Rojas m. 24-04-1884 in Guadalajara.
6 José López Portillo y Weber b. 19-04-1889 in Guadalajara
+Refugio Pacheco y Villa Gorda m. 13-10-1913 in Guadalajara
7 José López Portillo y Pacheco b. 16-06-1920 in Mexico City, Mexico
+Carmen Romano y Nolk m. 20-10-1951 in Mexico City
5 María Weber Narváez
+Carlos Fernando de Landero

4 María Nieves Josefa b 05-08-1839
+Julio Bertrand m. 28-09-1864 in Tepic
4 Joséfa Dolores Narváez b. 19-03-1841
4 Rito José María Narváez b. 22-05-1842
4 Leonides Dolores Narváez b. 08-08-1843
4 Eugenio Narváez b. 24-06-1844
4 Pedro Eugenio Narváez b. 30-06-1845
4 Manuela Narváez b. 29-10-1847
+Carlos Kofahl
5 Blanca Kofahl Narváez
+Luis Labastida Izquierdo
6 Julio Labastida Kofahl
+Alicia Martin del Campo
7 Julio Labastida Martin del Campo
*2nd spouse of Blanca Kofahl Narváez:
+Francisco Labastida Izquierdo
4 María Narváez Labastida b. 10-11-1857
3 María Simona de los Angeles Narváez b. 27-10-1803
3 Pedro Nolasco Antonio José María Narváez b. 30-11-1806
3 José María Pedro de Jesus Narváez b. 18-01-1809
3 José Ramon Nepomuceno b. 19-11-1811

Note: Bold numbers indicate José María Narváez' direct descendants to José López Portillo, former President of Mexico.

Bibliography

Alamán, Lucas. *Historia de México desde los primeros movimientos que prepararon su independencia en el año 1808 hasta la época presente.* 1st ed. 5 vols. Mexico City, 1849-52

Alvarez, Jose Rogelio. *Enciclopedia de México.* Mexico City: Secretary of Public Education 1988. Vol. 10, 5715

Anna, Timothy E. *The Mexican Empire of Iturbide.* Lincoln, Nebraska: University of Nebraska Press, 1990

Archer, Christon I. "Rebellion in the Rebellion of New Spain: The Indian Insurgents of Mezcala Island on the Lake Chapala Front, 1812-1816." Calgary: University of Calgary, Alta., 1994

———. "Russians, Indians & Passages: Spanish Voyages in Alaska in the 18th Century." *Explorations in Alaska.* Antoinette Shalkop (ed.). Anchorage, Alaska: Cook Inlet Historical Society 1980. 129-43

———. "Seduction before Sovereignty: Spanish Efforts to Manipulate the Natives in their Claims to the Northwest Coast." Paper delivered at The Vancouver Conference on Exploration & Discovery, Vancouver, B.C., April 1992

———. "Spanish Exploration and Settlement of the Northwest Coast in the 18th Century." In *Nutka.* Barbara S. Efrat and W. J. Langlois (ed.). Victoria, British Columbia: Province of British Columbia, 1978. 33-53

———. "The Transient Presence: A Re-Appraisal of Spanish Attitudes toward the Northwest Coast in the Eighteenth Century." *B.C. Studies* #18. University of British Columbia: UBC Press, Summer 1973. 3 ff.

Bartroli, Tomas. *Discovery of the Site of Vancouver City by José María Narváez in 1791.* A tentative account. Revised version made October 1986. Located in Special Collections Division, University of British Columbia Library, Vancouver, B.C.

Bartroli, Tomas. *Brief Presence: Spain's Activity on America's Northwest Coast (1774-1796).* Vancouver, British Columbia: Bartroli, 1991

Bateson, Ian (illustrator). "Vancouver, on the Move." Documentary film. Vancouver, British Columbia: Thomas Howe Associates, 1984

Bawlf, Sam. "Drake beat Cook and the rest . . ." *Vancouver Sun*, January 27, 1966. A17

Bodega y Quadra, Juan Francisco. *Carta General de cuanto hasta hoy se ha descubierto y examinado por los españoles en la Costa Septentríonal de California . . . por D. Juan Francisco de la Bodgega y Cuadra de la órden de Santiago, Capitan de Navio de la Real Armada y Comandante del Departamento.* 1791

Cardenas de la Peña, Enrique. *San Blas de Nayarit.* Mexico, City: Secretaria de Marina, 1968. Vol. 1: 134, 138; Vol. 2: 104, 117-120; 197-199

Chapman, Fredrik H. *Architectura Nalis Mercatoria 1768.* New York: 1967

Cook, Warren L. *Flood Tide of Empire: Spain and the Pacific Northwest, 1543-1819.* New Haven & London: Yale University Press, 1973

Colnett, James. *The Journals of Captain James Colnett aboard the Argonaut from April 26, 1789 to November 3, 1791.* Toronto: Champlain Society, 1940

Crosse, John. "Spaniards in the Gulf." *Boat World*, May 1991

———. "Day the Spanish Came Ashore." *Vancouver Sun*, July 17, 1991

Cruz, Francisco Santiago. *Fronteras con Rusia.* Mexico City: Editorial Jus, S.A., 1967. 83-85

Cutter, Donald C. *Malaspina and Galiano: Spanish Voyages to the Northwest Coast, 1791 & 1792.* Vancouver, British Columbia, 1991

———. "Jose Cardero: Protoartist of the Pacific Coast." Paper delivered at The Vancouver Conference on Exploration & Discovery, Vancouver, April 1992

———. *Malaspina in California.* San Francisco, 1960

Davis, Chuck. "José María Narváez." *The Province*, March 30, 1980

Duflot de Mofras, Eugene. *Exploration du Territoire de L'Orégon, des Californies et de la Mer Vermeille.* Paris 1844, 1846

———. *Travels on the Pacific Coast.* 2 vols. Translated and edited by Marguerite Eyer Wilbur. Santa Ana, California, 1937

Eliot, John L. "Alaska's Island Refuge." *National Geographic*, November 1993

Garcia de Alba, Gabriel Agraz. *Un Gaditano Insigne en America: Don José María Narbáez, explorador y cartografo de Alaska, de California y del primer mapa de Jalisco.* Mexico: Real Academia Hispanoamericana de Ciencias Artes y Letras, 1979

Hamill, Hugh M., Jr. *The Hidalgo Revolt: Prelude to Mexican Independence.* Gainesville, Florida: University of Florida, 1966

Harbron, John D. *Trafalgar and the Spanish Navy.* London: Conway, 1988

Henry, John Frazier. *Early Maritime Artists of the Pacific North west Coast, 1741-1841.* Vancouver: Douglas & McIntyre, 1984

Higueras, Maria Dolores. *Northwest Coast of America; Iconographic Album of the Malaspina Expedition.* Madrid: Museo Naval, 1991

Howay, Frederick William (editor). *Voyages of the "Columbia" to the Northwest Coast, 1787-1790 and 1790-1793.* Boston: Massachusetts Historical Society, 1941

Hull, Raymond and Soules, Gordon and Christine. *Vancouver's Past.* Seattle: University of Washington Press, 1974

Inglis, Robin, ed. *Spain and the North Pacific Coast.* Vancouver, British Columbia: Vancouver Maritime Museum, 1992

Kendrick, John. "Spaniards on the West Coast." *The Beaver*, June-July, 1987

———. *The Men with Wooden Feet.* Toronto: NC Press, 1985

———. trans. *The Voyage of Sutil and Mexicana, 1792.* Spokane, Washington: Arthur Clark Co., 1991

Kenyon, Malcolm Hall. "Naval Construction and Repair in San Blas." Master's thesis, University of New Mexico, 1972

Khlebnikov, Kiril. *Russkaia America v neopublikovannykh zapiskakh K. T. Khlebnikova.* Leningrad: Nauka, 1979

Lamb, William Kaye. "The Mystery of Mrs. Barkley's Diary. Notes on the Voyage of the *'Imperial Eagle,'* 1786-87." *British Columbia Historical Quarterly* #6. Victoria: Archives of B.C. and B.C. Historical Association, 1942

———. ed. *The Voyage of George Vancouver 1791-1795.* London: Hakluyt Society, 1984

McDowell, Jim. "Europeans on the Gran Canal." *Pacific Yachting*, April 1991

Marina de Guerra. *Estado de los méritos y servicios del Primer Piloto, Graduado de Alférez de Navio de la Real Armada Don José María Narváez, de Edad de 63 años, Estada Casado y sus servicios los siguientes.* Madrid: Archivo-Museo Don Alvaro de Bazan [Museo Naval]

Martínez, Estevan José. *Diario de Esteban José Martínez, 1788.* Mexico City: Archives of the Gabinete de Historia Natural [A.G.I.] (presently the Archivo del Museo Ciencias Naturales [A.M.C.N.].) Leg., 1529

———. *Diario de la Navegacion que Yo el Alf(ére)z de Navio de la R(ea)l Arm(a)da D(o)n Estevan Josef Martínez boy a executar al P(uer)to de S(a)n Lorenzo de Nuca, mandando la Frag(a)ta Princessa, y Paquebot S(a)n Carlos...1789.* Ed. by Roberto Barreiro-Meiro and titled *Coleccion de Diarios y Relaciones para la Historia de los Viajes y Descubrimientos.* Madrid: Instituto Histórico de Marina, 1964.

———. *Diary of the Voyage, in command of the frigate Princessa and the packet San Carlos in the present year of 1789.* Translation by William L. Schurz. Madrid: 1900. Located in Special Collections Library, University of British Columbia, Vancouver

———. *A translation of the Diary of Estevan José Martínez from July 2 till July 14, 1789 in The Journals of Captain James Colnett Aboard the Argonaut from April 26, 1789 to November 3, 1791.* Ed. by F.W. Howay. Toronto: 1940

Mathes, Michael W. "The Province of Anian and its Strait: Myth, Reality and Exploration of the Pacific Northwest, 1542-1792." Paper delivered at The Vancouver Conference on Exploration & Discovery, Vancouver, British Columbia, April 1992

Matthews, J.S. "Narváez 1791; Discoverer of the Boca de Florida Blanca." *Vancouver Historical Journal* #4. Vancouver, British Columbia: Archives of Vancouver Society, January 1961

———. "150th Anniversary 1791-1941 Sesquicentennial of the Arrival of First European on Pacific Mainland Shore of Canada at English Bay, Vancouver." Northwest Collection, Vancouver Public Library, Vancouver, British Columbia, 1941

Meares, John. *Voyages Made in the Years 1788 and 1789 from China to the Northwest Coast of America.* Amsterdam: N. Israel; New York: Da Capo, 1967

Mourelle de la Rúa, Francisco Antonio. *Voyage of the Sonora in the second Bucareli expedition to explore the Northwest Coast...* Translation of Mourelle's journal by Hon. Daines Barrington. [Includes reproduction of Bodega's *Carta General...*, showing Spanish discoveries on the coast up to 1791.] San Francisco: Thomas C. Russell, 1920

Narváez, José María. *Diario el Navegacion que Espera Haser el 2nd Piloto de la Real Armada Don José María Narbáez en el Paquebot el S.M. Nombrado el San Carlos comandado por el 1st Piloto López de Haro . . . , 1788.* William Andrews Clark Memorial Library, University of California Los Angeles. (Original, only one in existence, 32 leaves or 61 pages. Photocopies of original located in Provincial Archives of British

Columbia, Victoria, and Vancouver Public Library, Vancouver, British Columbia. Translation from Spanish by Jim McDowell located in Vancouver Public Library, Vancouver, British Columbia)

Navarrete, Martin Fernandez de. Introduction to *El Viage las Goletas Sutil y Mexicano.* Translation from Spanish in 1911 by G.F. Barwick, Keeper of Printed Books in the British Museum, is available in manuscript form in University of British Columbia Library and in the Provincial Archives in Victoria, British Columbia. Translation by Espinoza titled *Accounts of the Voyage Made by the Schooners Sutil and Mexicana in the Year 1792 to Survey the Strait of Fuca; with an Introduction Containing a Notice of the Expeditions Previously Carried out by the Spaniards in Search of the Northwest Passage of America.* Madrid: Royal Printing Office, 1802. Located in Northwest History Room of Vancouver Public Library, Vancouver, British Columbia

Novo y Colson, Pedro de, ed. *Viaje politico-cientifico alrededor del Mundo por las corbetas Descubierta y Atrevida.* 2 vols. Madrid: 1885. Translated by Carl Robinson and titled *Politico-Scientific Voyage Round the World by the Corvettes Descubierta and Atrevida under the Command of the Naval Captains Don Alexandro Malaspina and Don Jose de Bustamente y Guerra from 1789-1794.* Vancouver, British Columbia, 1934

Orozco y Berra, Manuel. *Apendice al Diccionario Universal de Historia y de Geografia.* Mexico: J.M. Audrade and F. Escalante, 1856. Vol. 3, 7-9

Otero, Mariano. *Obras del Sr. Licenciado Mariano Otero.* Edited by his son Ignacio Otero. Mexico: Tipografia de Nabor Chavez, 1859. 62-63

Palacios, Antonio. *Diario de Antonio Palacios, 1788.* Biblioteca Nacional, Mexico

Serantes, Antonio. *Diario de Antonio Serantes, 1788.* Biblioteca Nacional, Mexico

Szewczyk, David. *The Viceroyalty of New Spain and Early Independent Mexico: A Guide to Original Manuscripts in the Collections of The Rosenbach Museum and Library.* Philadelphia: Rosenbach Museum and Library, 1980

Thelander, Carl G. *Life on the Edge: A Guide to California's Endangered National Resources.* Santa Cruz, California: Biosystems Books, 1994

Thurman, Michael E. *The Naval Department of San Blas: New Spain's Bastion for Alta California and Nootka, 1767-1798.* Glendale, California: Arthur H. Clark Co., 1967

Wagner, Henry Raup. *Cartography of the Northwest Coast of America.* Berkeley: University of California Press, 1937

———. *Spanish Explorations in the Strait of Juan de Fuca.* New York: Fine Arts Press 1933, AMS Press, 1971

———. *Spanish Voyages to the Northwest Coast of America in the Sixteenth Century.* San Francisco: California Historical Society, 1929

Williams, Glyndwr. "Myth and Reality: The Theoretical Geography of Northwest America from Cook to Vancouver." Paper delivered at The Vancouver Conference on Exploration and Discovery, Vancouver, British Columbia, April 1992

Wilson, Iris Higbie. *Noticias de Nutka, An Account of Nootka Sound in 1792.* Seattle: University of Washington Press, 1970

Index

José Narváez
The Forgotten Explorer
has been printed in an edition of 750 copies.
The typeface is Caslon.
Typesetting by Barbara Moore, designed by Robert Clark.
Printing and binding by Braun-Brumfield, Inc.,
Ann Arbor, Michigan.